WARRIOR
of the
RAINBOW

A gay former Catholic priest
journeys from his secret to freedom.

RAY BUTEAU

Published by
Hasmark Publishing
www.hasmarkpublishing.com

Disclaimer

This book is designed to provide information and motivation to our readers. It is sold with the understanding that the publisher is not engaged to render any type of psychological, legal, or any other kind of professional advice. The content of each article is the sole expression and opinion of its author, and not necessarily that of the publisher. No warranties or guarantees are expressed or implied by the publisher's choice to include any of the content in this volume. Neither the publisher nor the individual author(s) shall be liable for any physical, psychological, emotional, financial, or commercial damages, including, but not limited to, special, incidental, consequential or other damages. Our views and rights are the same: You are responsible for your own choices, actions, and results.

Permission should be addressed in writing to Ray Buteau at warrioroftherainbow@outlook.com

Editor: Corinne L. Casazza
corinnecasazza@gmail.com

Cover & Book Design: Anne Karklins
anne@hasmarkpublishing.com

ISBN 13: 978-1-989161-82-1
ISBN 10: 1989161820

Hasmark
PUBLISHING

WARRIOR OF THE RAINBOW

One can't see the overall bigger picture of one's life and destiny. One can only have faith that a loving God (however one understands a God to be) is directing one's life, which I've always had.

In 1994 when an Aboriginal Elder called me to be a Warrior of the Rainbow, I had no idea what that meant, nor did I ask him at the time. I just thought 'that sounds interesting' and left it at that. I wouldn't think of it till years later as I would hear of what 'warrior' meant to different people. Then I'd remember what the Elder had said to me.

As the years went by, the name meant more to me and I began to see that it may have a greater significance in my life. As I matured, an understanding of what it meant for me unfolded. In 2006, that calling to be a Warrior of the Rainbow revealed itself to me again when I was reading *The E-Myth Revisited*. In it, Michael Gerber quotes Don Juan in *Tales of Power*: "The basic difference between an ordinary man and a warrior is that a warrior takes everything as a challenge while an ordinary man takes everything either as a blessing or a curse."

For many in the Aboriginal culture "Warrior of the Rainbow" refers to those who are fighting for mankind's reconnection to Mother Earth. But for me it meant the challenges we all face throughout our spiritual journeys. And the word 'rainbow' had the significance of the passages, the 'transitions' that we all go through. So, for me the name 'Warrior of the Rainbow' is my calling to journey with those facing the challenges in their life transitions. The challenges that face other gay Catholic priests, women who live as enablers in codependent relationships as did I as a priest, and to those who are the 'outsiders, not fitting in,' other members of the Rainbow (LGBTQ) community, and to all who are moving beyond religiosity in their spiritual lives.

To my brother
Gaetan

CONTENTS

ACKNOWLEDGMENTS

To my parents, siblings, relatives, friends, educators:
THANK YOU

For my parish ministry, chaplaincy, editors, proof-readers,
publisher of 'No Longer Lonely' and 'Those in Power:'
THANK YOU

For the Monroe Institute, Bob Proctor & Associates:
THANK YOU

and
NAMASTE
(may our spirits remain united)

FOREWORD

Secrets can be dangerous, especially if you're a gay priest. They can be doubly dangerous if you're a gay priest who happens to be ministering to prisoners at Manitoba's Headingley Correctional Centre. Ray Buteau discovered that painful lesson when a new prisoner spotted him as a long-forgotten one-night fling from the outside.

The year was 2002 and Buteau was expelled from the priesthood. He had served the Church for 25 years. For all those years, he had helped others by offering spiritual solace in their dark moments. And during all that time he had lived in painful isolation and loneliness, unable to express his true self.

Buteau had entered the priesthood out of a real desire to serve God. It was also a way to avoid having to get into relationships with women. As Buteau puts it: "God would take care of my abnormal thoughts and deeds." That's not how it worked out.

INTRODUCTION

I will always remember the day my sister Carole asked me "Ray, why would God call you to be a priest knowing that you're gay?"

To answer that I had to ask myself: *Why was I born into our family?*

In order to live a "normal gay life" with a God of unconditional love, I needed a spirituality outside the religious box that I had been born into. I needed to transcend that box and discover my true self.

My spirituality has become a harmonious relationship with myself — body, mind and spirit — as well as with others, and with God. When I speak of God, I speak of divine energy and infinite presence. For you, I respect however you understand God to be.

In summer of 2019 I turn 75 and with Leonard Cohen as my model, will begin a new stage in my life giving a voice to my spiritual journey.

1

SELF-ACCEPTANCE

One's sexual orientation was not discussed in good Catholic families in the 1960s and 70s. It was not discussed in elementary school or high school, and certainly not in Catholic seminary or amongst straight, ordained priests or with parishioners. Yet, sexuality is always a big issue, particularly amongst adolescents, and especially amongst the precocious youth of that era. In "proper" families, sexual orientation, particularly if you were not "straight," was so beyond "big issue" that it was best kept secret... like a personal fault or shameful character flaw.

The 'Outing' — Part 1

Headingley Correctional Centre is a few miles west of Winnipeg. The kilometre or so drive down the scenic and serene road off the Trans-Canada Highway is a stark contrast to life inside the institution's walls. In summer, it's lined with trees and well-cut lawns, often rabbits and deer graze within easy sight. I frequently slowed down to let them pass. In winter, the sun sparkles off a blanket of snow that pretty much covers everything as far as the eye can see.

On that traumatic day of my life, the drive in from the highway was remarkably still and silent. As the car approached the checkpoint halfway between the highway and the centre, the duty officer recognized me as a staff member, nodded, and waved me through. Once parked, I plugged in the car, hung my parking pass on the rearview mirror, locked up and walked toward the front door.

A white limousine was parked there and I thought at first that someone special must be visiting. But then the prison doors opened and an inmate, a gang member, walked out and headed for the limo. With a lot of the other inmates watching, he climbed in and it drove off. The practice, while certainly popular with the inmates, has since been stopped.

I buzzed the front door and waited to be identified via an overhead camera. The cameras were everywhere, constantly observing everyone. A loud buzz let me through the first door, but I had to wait a few seconds for the outside door to close before the next heavy steel door would open.

Instantly, I heard the clashing of steel doors, the sounds of officers shouting orders and the foul language from inmates as they passed one another in the halls. The strong smell of bacon grease greeted my arrival. Inmates were coming and going from the cafeteria with complaints about the food, the coffee, the amount they received or the little time they had to eat it. For every meal, every day, they had the same complaints, always with the same strong odour of grease as a backdrop.

Down the hallway, I stopped to sign in and greet the guards on duty.

"Good morning Father Ray," they always replied.

From there, I buzzed another set of barred doors and was let into the main hallway. Once inside, I tried to avoid colliding with the chaos — others coming and going, trays of food being brought to segregated areas, inmates in chains being escorted to court hearings, outside appointments or family funerals.

"Hey chaplain, I need to see you soon," someone shouted.

"Fill out a request form," I shouted back.

Two flights of stairs lead to the Spiritual Care Department with its four offices: one for an aboriginal elder; one for the chaplain, who is the department head; mine; and a spare office for interviews. There's also a chapel area that seats fifty, a classroom used by interns studying clinical pastoral education and a lounge area where the chaplains meet.

I greeted my co-worker and no sooner had I settled into my office and started going through my list of inmate requests when the phone rang. The call was from Mike, the newly appointed head of provincial chaplains. "Good morning Ray," he said, "an urgent matter has come up and I need to come to the institution to speak to you about it."

"Oh… Okay," I said tentatively. "I'll be here… and look forward to meeting with you." Bewildered, I shared the news with my co-worker, who seemed both surprised and uncomfortable.

I asked him if he knew what it could be about and he said he had no idea. While we waited for Mike, my co-worker made some coffee and I went down to the cafeteria to see if I could get some pastries.

When Mike arrived, formalities were dealt with more quickly than usual; he seemed in a hurry to speak to me. I absentmindedly asked if my co-worker could join us, not realizing how personal the issue was, and Mike anxiously agreed to have him present.

"I'm sorry to inform you that a sexual accusation has been made against you, Ray," he blurted as soon as the door was shut. "I've notified the superintendent and your bishop."

I looked at my co-worker in shock and embarrassment and wondered why he was allowed to witness my humiliation. I later discovered that everyone except me had already known the subject at hand.

"What's this all about?" I asked in total disbelief. I had never received any notification of an accusation. When I learned that even the superintendent and my bishop had been notified before me, I was numb with disbelief.

My co-worker watched in silence as Mike asked me if I knew a certain inmate named Steve.

"Yes," I said, "I met with him after he arrived a few weeks ago."

I had been asked to see that particular inmate and, after speaking with him and hearing his story, he had looked at me and said, "You don't recognize me do you, Father Ray?"

"No, I'm sorry, I don't... have we met?"

He proceeded to describe my apartment in detail and the one-night stand we'd had a few years before.

"I'm sorry if knowing who I am is a problem for you," I told him with a calmness that surprised even me. "Under the circumstances," I went on, "I need to notify my co-worker about this... it might be better for you to see him instead of me."

"I'd feel more comfortable seeing you," Steve said, "since you know who I am and what I'll have to deal with here."

"I'm willing to see you, but I need to notify my co-worker about the situation anyway."

My co-worker had been my supervisor during clinical training, and I think he considered himself a friend. He knew me better than most and was always aware and supportive of my orientation, as long as it was not an issue for me in what could be a very dangerous environment. I assured him that it had not been an issue during my parish ministry and was not an issue at the prison.

"So, what do you want to do?" My co-worker had asked at the time.

"I know how he has to be and how difficult it will be for him in this environment. Even though we have obviously had a sexual encounter, I can honestly say I don't remember him. As horrible as that may sound, it's not unusual for a one-night stand. He'd like to continue seeing me while he's here, but I don't know how you feel about that."

"I'll have a talk with him and let you know," he said, Later, my co-worker told me he thought Steve understood that I should not continue to meet with him for spiritual care.

"What am I being accused of?" I ask the provincial chaplain.

He explained in graphic detail an intense sexual encounter, which supposedly had been videotaped and, according to the chaplain as well, had gone on for a few days.

"I admit I probably had an encounter with this man because he knows my apartment in detail, but I deny having done any of those masochistic activities or having a camera on and I'm prepared to take a lie detector test to prove it."

But I was guilty by accusation; those in authority had been notified and my fate was sealed.

"You'll have to see your bishop, who has been notified," the chaplain added. "You won't be able to keep your position here as chaplain without his endorsement and, of course, you need to speak to the superintendent as soon as possible, before this gets out in the institution."

I couldn't believe what was happening and what was being said. It all hit me hard! There had been no warning, only a complete disregard for normal protocol in dealing with sensitive, personnel matters. And it was all stated in such a matter of fact, guilt-assumed manner it took my breath away.

Then, with a curt, "Sorry about all this Ray... good luck to you," the provincial chaplain was out the door.

My co-worker looked agitated as he said he would be supportive and suggested I see the superintendent.

"Is this true Ray," the superintendent asked?

"It's true that I probably did have a sexual encounter with the guy, though I don't remember him... but the details are false... I'm willing to take a lie detector test."

"Ray, I'll take your word for it," he said, "and I'll have the inmate transferred immediately, before things start being said. We need an endorsement from your bishop for you to keep your position here."

As I listened to him, still in disbelief, he went on.

"I suggest you go and see him as soon as possible and report back to me. You need to deal with this now."

And with that, my schedule for the next month took a drastic change.

The bishop, of course, was expecting my call. It was 2002; he was new to our diocese and not in the mood for anything remotely similar to the priest/pedophile scandals that were hitting the media at the time and could put him in the spotlight. He was direct, to say the least.

"Are you living a celibate life?"

"No, Bishop, I am not."

"Then you're to stop your lifestyle and live the chaste life you have been called to live, is that clear?" he narrowed his eyes at me.

"The only thing that isn't clear, Bishop, is whether I can live a celibate life. I'm questioning my calling to the priesthood."

"In that case, I'm sure you've heard of Southdown (a psychological treatment centre north of Toronto). I am sending you there for an evaluation and assessment of your ability to live a chaste, celibate life."

As he shook my hand goodbye, he added, "You'll be contacted in a few days; be prepared to leave for a week's evaluation."

With a bishop, there is seldom a choice about whether you want to do something or not, only ultimatums.

The following day, I got a call telling me that I had a flight to Toronto on Sunday and would be picked up at the airport when I landed. I had two days to notify the superintendent and a few friends and to get myself ready.

Sunday evening, I arrived in Toronto and headed for the airport exit to find the white limo and chauffeur that were waiting for me.

The Early Years

"Where are you going to plant those trees Dad?"

"One is going in the front yard, and the other in the back."

Being only six years old, the eight-foot twigs looked very high when Dad stood them up; more like long poles than trees because they had few branches. The root ends were wrapped in sackcloth bags, which Dad left on them as he put them directly into the holes he had dug, then he untied the bags and filled in the holes with topsoil. We patted and stomped the earth around the base of the trunk to make sure it was solidly in place.

"Water those trees every day and they'll live and grow... don't, and they won't," he pronounced as he stood back to appreciate his efforts.

We watered them every day and waited for signs of life. Finally, buds appeared and opened, and in the fall, after the few leaves that had been produced that year had turned crimson and fell to the ground, Dad wrapped the branches in cloth to protect them through their first winter.

As spring approached, I checked those trees daily for signs of life. When they appeared in the form of small buds that seemed to double in size every day, I was amazed and felt a kinship to those scrawny trees. As the days and weeks passed, the buds grew, slowly opening into hundreds of leaves that covered every branch as it stretched out to do its part in forming a beautifully full red maple. I loved those trees from the day we planted them and felt peace just being near them. Dad said they were nice but really just reminded him of his second most favourite NHL hockey team and how poorly they were doing.

Unlike my Dad, my male friends and I were not the least interested in hockey, or sports of any kind, though we did play a version of soft ball in the backyard on occasion. We preferred playing and trading marbles, making forts, wrestling around on the lawn, and just hanging out.

When I wrestled with another boy on the thick green grass of our lawn and held him down, or squeezed him in a headlock, his warmth, his scent and closeness felt good to me, even excited me, though I didn't understand why.

It often happened that when I had one of them in a good neck hold or was on top of him, Mom would shout at me, "Ray, it's time to come in now." And when Mom said "now," she meant, "NOW!"

She didn't seem to like my male friends. Though she never said so outright, she did ask a few times why I liked playing with them so much. Sensing that she didn't approve, I didn't have the courage to tell her that they made me feel good. She never stopped me from playing with female friends, even when we were in a tent made with blankets in the backyard or alone in the basement. But with my female friends, I felt nothing special at all.

Perhaps Mom suspected something was amiss with me and other boys. Maybe it was just that more of my male friends were not Catholics. According to her and my Dad, unless my friends converted and became Roman Catholic before they died, they couldn't go to heaven. Even at six years old, I couldn't understand that because I really liked my male friends and their parents. But my parents, along with the priests at church and the nuns at school, all believed it, so it had to be true.

Dad was particularly unshakeable. What the Pope said, God agreed with. And what Dad said about God, we believed, like "Water those trees every day and they'll grow, don't, and they won't." I could understand and believe that, so I thought his other pronouncements must be true too. Yet, deep down in my stomach, it didn't feel right that God would make my friends go to hell simply because they were not Catholic. It just didn't make sense to me.

Nothing was more important to my parents than being Roman Catholic. I remember a new high school was being built in our neighborhood but the Catholic high school, which my parents and the Catholic community expected me to attend, was in the southern part of the city and included an expensive tuition fee with uniforms. My parents weren't ready for the tuition and extra expenses, so I got to attend the new high school in the opposite direction, in Protestant territory no less.

The school was a hot bed of activity and energy. It was the 1960s and the environment was exciting. Though shy and timid, my new male friends and I actually became the "in-crowd" and soon attracted female friends. They all lived in very nice homes and had things that I didn't, like their own bedrooms with their own radios, record players, records, magazines and posters on their walls.

Except for some of the major sports, we got involved in every school activity: the school choir, drama class, camera and social clubs, the curling team, the yearbook club, and were even elected to the student council.

The 60s were the time of the Beatles and Beatlemania, psychedelic music, Bob Dylan and Simon and Garfunkel. We danced the twist and the monkey. I loved dancing and had a natural sense of rhythm. Girls wore miniskirts and tall leather boots and guys wore paisley shirts, bright, bold colours and tight, very tight, velvet trousers revealing every crack and bulge. And, of course, we all had long hair. The look was a mixture of oriental, African, space-age and hippie. We went to the movies a lot, seeing *Psycho, Spartacus, Exodus* and *Where the Boys Are.*

It was also the dawning of the age of television and we watched *The Andy Griffith Show, Candid Camera, The Jack Benny Show, Dennis the Menace, My Three Sons, The Ed Sullivan Show, Perry Mason, Bonanza, The Red Skelton Show* and *Alfred Hitchcock Presents.*

But, by the end of tenth grade, my parents were feeling a lot of pressure from the Sunday announcements at church telling them to send their children to the "right" school. I didn't like the idea of being separated from my friends, but I knew my parents believed my going to a Catholic school was important for me, so I did.

Religious education classes were more like health classes. We studied what we couldn't and shouldn't do with our bodies. I soon began to understand another reason why my parents might have wanted me to go to that school — we'd be talking about the one topic that they never talked about — sex! I quickly learned that sex and sin were closely related.

Religious education was taught by a teaching order of priests, the Holy Cross Fathers. These men were fun to talk to and very serious about their faith. One early class that immediately got everyone's attention began with the Father pronouncing:

"Today we are going to speak about a very serious mortal sin, which we need to control in our lives."

"Sounds interesting," I thought as I, and everyone else in the class, fixed their eyes on him.

"And that's masturbation," he continued.

Masturbation was a normal part of our development, he admitted, but also a mortal sin! It was not meant for our carnal pleasure; it had to be controlled and should be confessed. Other guys chuckled as the priest spoke, but not me. My heart rate quickened, and I could feel my face flush as I realized I had frequently been committing a mortal sin and didn't even know it. I don't think I heard anything else the priest said in that class.

That year, though I was no longer wrestling with my male friends, I felt even more attracted to them. I was surrounded by guys in tight jeans and, even when they wore blazers, their front bulge was obvious. I didn't understand why I felt the way I did. In those days we never spoke about gays. I didn't know anything about homosexuality. I thought my sexual attraction to men was something peculiar only to me; I didn't know why I thought and felt the way I did. I was terrified of what might happen to me if someone found out.

I tried praying the thoughts away, but that only stalled the inevitable because my imagination would be re-activated the second I came across a guy who was well built — not to mention the effect gym classes had on me. I had to be very careful not to be caught looking below the belt. So, I fantasized, masturbated and went to confession.

Actor Steve McQueen became a kind of fantasy lover. Seeing him in movies or magazines always aroused me to masturbate. I didn't know why, but I knew it was a serious mortal sin. I felt there was something very wrong with me. I was afraid if my mother found out she would send me away somewhere to get treated. I thought of speaking to one of the priests about it, but feared he would tell my parents, or worse, try to get me to tell them myself.

As it was, any communication with my mother was difficult at best. And when she was angry or, for some reason, annoyed with me about something, she would go off to her ironing, or sewing, or read her newspaper rather than talk with me about whatever it was.

"Mom, what's the matter?" I'd ask, and she would quickly put her hand out toward me, motioning me to stop.

"I don't want to talk about it," she'd say.

I always knew I'd hurt her feelings when she gave me that silent, glaring look that seemed to go right through me. Other times, when I wanted to go out somewhere, she'd ask, "Why are you always going out? Why don't you stay home once in awhile?"

And if I was relaxing at home, watching TV or reading, she'd ask, "Why don't you go and visit someone instead of just sitting around all the time?"

Staying in Mom's good favour meant doing the dishes without being asked and taking care of my brother and sisters. To her credit, when I was younger she tried to get me interested in the accordion, which I could hardly hold, but then she did get me into tap dancing, which I excelled at. The music, the satin, studded costumes, the makeup, the lights, the applause; it all excited me.

My parents, and even my friends, could tell something was bothering me in those latter high school days. "What's the matter Ray?" Mom would ask, and I would echo back, "It's nothing; I don't want to talk about it." That was usually the limit of conversations with Mom, but not with God.

The thought that masturbation, which felt normal and pleasurable to me, was somehow displeasing to God just didn't make sense. I had always thought of myself as a good and caring person and wasn't trying to disobey Him, or anyone. I just couldn't accept that

God was unconditional love and at the same time would judge me and condemn me to hell for this mortal sin.

Why would God even care if I masturbated? Was the church telling God what was right and wrong? Was God just going along with what the church was teaching us? If I didn't confess my mortal sin and died, would God go along with what they were saying and condemn me to eternity in hell?

Everyone was telling me that that was what our faith taught and what God was asking of me. Increasingly, I felt I was left with no choices.

One day, on my knees in the school chapel, I said to God, "In my heart I know what I'm being taught is not right, and that I won't be condemned for what I'm doing. I'll continue to confess it, just in case, but I know that if I die I'm not going to hell."

God kept my secret.

Later that year, I was persuaded to take part in a school skit for a fundraising event.

When I accepted, I hadn't known I'd be playing the part of one of our school teachers, a priest. My parents didn't know what role I had. I asked them one day if they would tell me how my costume looked and see if it needed any alterations. They agreed, and I got dressed.

As I came out of the bedroom looking like a Holy Cross Father, they gasped.

"Wait a minute!" Mom exclaimed as she quickly went for the camera. The seed had been planted.

After that year, I wanted out of Catholic school and to go back to being with my friends at the regular high school. My parents saw that I had really been struggling with my grades and would have to take summer classes to be accepted into Grade 12, so they agreed to the change.

Back with my friends at Lakeport with all its new facilities, including a large gymnasium that was perfect for school dances, I noticed quite a change in the guys. They were forever talking about girls and wanting parties so they could have those slow, close, cheek-to-cheek, body to-body dances. I much preferred rock and roll.

To add fuel to the fire, we decided that when there wasn't a school dance we'd take turns hosting a weekend dance party at each other's homes. All we needed were balloons, streamers, coke, chips, a full punch bowl, a record player, lots of records and a volunteer to keep them playing. We notified all our neighbours and invited their kids if they were our age and told everyone when the party would end. My parents liked our group and welcomed us. In fact, if Mom hadn't nudged Dad to leave, he probably would've stayed the whole evening to talk to everyone.

There was one girl that I liked as a friend and as a great dance partner. I felt safe and comfortable with her because I didn't feel I had to do anything intimate with her. She didn't seem to like the slow dances either. Though we did them, neither of us got excited by them. We both loved dancing and we needed room to move when we rock-and-rolled, danced the cha-cha, the polka and the twist. The monkey didn't require much room at all. She wasn't any more romantically interested in me than I was in her, so we got along well.

In fact, no one in the group seemed interested in dating or going steady, but the guys were interested in getting laid and tried to get me to go along with them on their bar pick-ups. I always had an excuse for not being available — usually some Catholic event. I just wasn't interested in girls in the same way they were, but I couldn't tell them that. They would want to know why and if I told them I'd lose them as friends. Trying to avoid the topic and the invitations to go out with them became very tiring.

More and more, my secret restricted my social life as the months went by. I tried to focus on my homework but as the year progressed, the pressures continued to build. My friends wondered why I wasn't joining in and I couldn't tell them why I wasn't interested, all of which made me wonder what I was going to do with my life. How

I was going to keep my secret, what kind of career did I want, or could I have? And still, I visited the confessional booth all too often. Something had to give.

The Call

Every year, as sure as buds reappear on the trees, a Catholic Sunday service is set aside in which all priests speak from the pulpit to encourage young men to think of a vocation in the priesthood. One particular "Vocation Sunday," I was forced to begin opening up like the buds when our newly ordained priest asked the question, "Have you ever thought of the priesthood?"

I hadn't... and he seemed to be speaking directly to me. I had never thought about giving my life to God. After all that God had done for me, I had never considered devoting my life to His service and felt tremendous guilt. The notion felt right, like God was guiding me, giving me a way out. As a priest I wouldn't have to worry about my sexual feelings, I'd receive a good education, and my friends and family would respect my choice of career. I was overcome with emotion.

It felt as if someone had just asked me a very important question, but I didn't know how to answer it. Why was I feeling close to tears? I was 20 years old, confused about my attraction to other men, unable to see myself settling down with a woman and I had no one to speak to about any of it.

When I arrived home that day, I saw the "Annals of St. Anne de Beaupre" on the living room coffee table alongside my mother's newspaper. I picked it up, sat on the couch, and began browsing through it. A picture of an old man in a light-tan, hooded garment looking serene, intent in prayer, caught my attention.

"Mom, who is this man?" I asked. "What's this about?"

"It's about Trappist Monks," she replied. "They're a cloistered order, spending their days in work and prayer and most of that in silence."

How very different, I thought.

I was familiar with Buddhist Monks but hadn't known that the Catholic Church also had monks.

Without telling anyone, I sent away for information and, a couple of weeks later, received an envelope with large red letters written across the top — "Trappist Monks."

"Are you seriously thinking about becoming a monk?" my mother asked as I stared at the envelope.

"I just wanted to know more about it," I said. "Do you remember that sermon when Father asked, 'Have you ever thought of the priesthood'?"

The question immediately secured her undivided attention.

"Well," I went on, "I've been thinking about it, but I'm not sure if I want to become a priest. I'm really bothered by how I feel and I don't know what to do about it."

Scarcely controlling her excitement, she said, "You should go and see the parish priest and talk to him about it."

I had to admit that choosing to become a monk seemed preferable to becoming a parish priest. I had always thought of parish priests as rather materialistic, living the good life with fancy cars, nice residences and even housekeepers. I felt called to a closer relationship with God but didn't understand what that might involve.

As the weeks went by, more envelopes started arriving from different religious communities: Dominicans, Franciscans, White Fathers, Jesuits, Redemptorists and many others.

Meanwhile, my grandmother Maillet didn't want to see me become a cloistered monk so she had my uncle send away for information from religious communities that offered seminary studies. One such community caught my attention, the Institute Voluntas Dei. Grandmother Maillet knew about it through the chaplain at her seniors' home and recommended it to me.

I was interested in their setup. I could go to the seminary and try it for a year to see if the lifestyle was for me. Because it was funded by benefactors and not the Catholic Church, I wouldn't have to be affiliated with any bishop.

However, in spite of the information I had, I was confused and unsure about what I wanted to do. I felt I had to speak to the priest who had raised the question. I called to arrange a meeting with him and went to the rectory a few days later. The young priest was very gracious, kind and supportive.

"I had never thought about having a closer relationship to God until you asked the question in your sermon," I told him.

"You seem quite troubled by this," he said, "and your emotions are, perhaps, a sign that God is calling you to the priesthood."

That made some sense to me but I wasn't convinced.

"But I haven't taken any Latin," I said, which was a requirement for seminary entrance.

"I'm willing to teach you Latin during the summer months," he suggested, "and, along with a tutor, I'll prepare you for the entrance exams."

I still wasn't convinced but I said, "If you're willing to do all this for me, I'm willing to try it for a year."

That summer, the trees Dad and I had planted when I was six were over 15 feet high, with a diameter of branches and red maple leaves just as wide. They provided comfort and refreshing shade for me while I studied my "Living Latin" textbook. Under their branches I not only felt protected from the heat of the sun, but also connected to something much bigger than me, to something universal and spiritual — to God.

At the end of that summer, I applied to the institute and was accepted. At the time, I knew nothing about homosexuality, or about the notion of coming out and living life as a gay man. I thought keeping my secret was my means of survival. The life-changing sermon and grandma's intervention were, for me, God's intervention, guiding and protecting me. Like many similarly oriented men, I was marrying to further protect my secret. But unlike straight men who married, it wouldn't be a woman with whom I'd find shelter.

Minor Seminary

I sat under the red maple tree in the back yard enjoying the warm summer evening. Thoughts of the day Dad and I had planted the tree so many years before triggered a flood of flashbacks of my childhood and teen years, of memories, good and bad, of times with Mom and Dad and my brother and sisters. A sad nostalgia battled with excitement about the future.

I wanted to enjoy the setting sun and the sound of the gentle breeze rustling through the leaves above me, but in the morning my parents were taking me to the bus depot and I knew I should go in and spend a little time with them before finishing my last-minute packing and heading for bed.

The next morning as the bus pulled away, my eyes stung with insistent tears, but it wasn't long before my mind dwelt less on the chapter of life I was closing and more on anticipation of the one I was opening. Before I knew it, we had arrived at the Institute Voluntas Dei Seminary in Trois Rivieres, Quebec and the pace quickened as I began the registration process.

My first surprise came quickly with news that I would have a roommate. Surprise number two was being introduced to him right then and there. My roommate, Pierre, looked very pleasant, indeed! The priest introduced us and asked him to show me to our room and help me settle in before supper.

As we made our way through the organized confusion, Pierre introduced me to students from all over the world. I was surprised to meet fellow seminarians from Sri Lanka, Trinidad, France, Laos and Haiti. The fraternity was striking, invigorating, as if everyone had known each other for years.

"All first and second-year students are bunked together," he said as we finally approached the dormitory. "Third-year students have their own rooms."

Our room had all the basics — two beds, desks, bookshelves, dressers and — Pierre! When it was time to call it a day, he had no problem taking off his clothes in front of me and lying on his bed in his underwear. He was six feet tall and muscular, with broad shoulders, a nice chest, strong arms and legs, and a nice butt. His light hair was thick and his eyes brown — definitely a good-looking young man to say the least. He wasn't a model, but he was close and, yes, I definitely noticed.

But I wasn't ready for him! Until that first night with Pierre, I'd had my fantasies about Steve McQueen, but here I was, my first night in the seminary with this six-foot, good-looking man laying before me in his underwear. I had a difficult time maintaining eye contact.

I put on my bathrobe before taking my underwear off to get into my pajamas. Although he didn't say anything, he must have found that process a little unusual. He probably thought I was shy, which would have been understating the obvious.

When we turned off the lights, I was ready for sleep but lay there for several minutes thinking about my day: leaving Mom and Dad, the trip, meeting students from all over the world and now, this good-looking guy lying on top of his sheets in his underwear.

Early the next morning I opened my eyes to see Pierre wrapping a towel around his naked body as he headed for the showers. There was no way I was going to the showers like that. After he left the room, I donned my bathrobe and was relieved when I opened the door to the hallway and saw other guys in bathrobes — carrying their towels instead of wearing them. I was more than a little relieved to find the showers consisted of rows of one-person stalls with doors.

I returned to my room shortly after and found Pierre drying himself with his towel. With my bathrobe still on, I slipped into my underwear and tried not to watch him. I certainly wanted to but was deathly afraid of him noticing me noticing him.

Instead, I looked out the window of our small room to the seminary beyond. It consisted of several buildings and was surrounded by a thick forest of spruce and maple trees cut with miles of winding trails. The view kept my attention off Pierre until I was ready to leave.

My first experience entering the woods around the seminary was both enchanting and emotional. My hometown was a beautiful city with its streets lined with oak and maple trees and parks with willows and spruce, but here the trees intermingled to form a tapestry of colours, shapes and sizes. Each step was an invitation to take another, and another, walking farther and farther into the calm, constantly comforted by the forest floor of ferns, small flowers and mushrooms.

Marshes scattered throughout the woods were filled with the sounds of frogs and birds. This world was alive, not only with all its many creatures including white-tailed deer, but also with something else, something even more enchanting, more mysterious than the forest itself. I couldn't name it at the time, but it left me overwhelmed with a sense of peacefulness. I felt no fear of any potential version of the big bad wolf or of getting lost because I was not alone — I was in a sacred place with God.

All of nature encircled and comforted me. I felt protected and safe to say or feel any emotion that came to the surface. Walking out of the woods made me feel like I was leaving someone behind, yet I knew He would be there when I returned.

Though the inside of a church had always been a very reverent place for me, it had never offered the same feeling of closeness to God that the woods did. In nature, I could look within myself and feel a relationship, a presence that offered me inner prayer and dialogue, and time alone with my God.

On our first Friday evening, a conference was held with Father Louis-Marie Parent, the founder of the institute presenting. I had met him briefly during the registration process. He spoke to us about spirituality and the spiritual framework of his institute, which he referred to as the 5-5-5. He had a sincere and kind presence about him and spoke passionately. He said 5-5-5 was an attitude to life and how we should view ourselves, our relationships with others and with God. It was a powerful concept that I immediately took to heart.

Father Parent explained that the first five has to do with our relationship with God: our intimacy with the Lord through daily prayer, centred on the spiritual exercises of mental prayer or meditation; reading the word of God (the scriptures); the Eucharist (mass); devotion to the blessed sacrament (hour adorations); and devotion to the Virgin Mary, especially through fervent meditation on the mysteries of the rosary.

The second five, he explained, is an inner attitude or spirit of contemplation, of humility and fraternal charity expressed and nurtured through an awareness of the presence of God. It's an absence of criticism and complaint, being of service and being peacemakers. The third five concerns our relationships with others. We are called to seize the opportunity every day to perform at least five concrete acts of charity to practise living with others in a positive manner, as Jesus taught us. We were not to be telling others that we were doing acts of charity for them; all that mattered was that we be aware that we were doing five acts of charity and of practising 5-5-5 every day.

A similar evening conference about teams was held on Saturday evening. We were divided into groups of five or six, along with a third-year student as a team leader. Teams would meet weekly and members were supposed to support each other. At our first team meeting we would be assigned a chore for the month, then another at the beginning of every month thereafter in a rotational cycle.

Other topics of weekly team meetings turned out to be how we were managing with our studies, spiritual exercises and subjects that we either wanted raised ourselves, or that the team leader or staff wanted us to discuss. Once a month, to keep up the team spirit, we'd go to a movie, out for a hike or to a restaurant or challenge another team to a sporting activity. When my team met for the first time, I thought we looked like the United Nations. I was Canadian, our group leader was from Sri Lanka, and the others were from France, Trinidad, Haiti and Laos.

At 9:45 the bells rang on the first Sunday morning. Cars were arriving with families that had come for Sunday mass, and with 60 students and 40 Oblate Sisters, we filled the church. It seemed like only a half hour later it was over, but more than an hour had passed. The solemnity of several priests celebrating together, with several seminarians as servers, and the contagious enthusiasm and the power of the singing almost brought me to tears. I was saddened to see it end.

In contrast, in my home parish our family had always attended the 9 a.m. mass. Here we had the parish priest, who had probably just gotten out of bed, two altar servers, myself having been one of them and the organist, who was accompanied by someone trying to lead a reluctant and unenthusiastic congregation in "How Great Thou Art" — a congregation that kept an eye on their watches, knowing it would be over soon and they could leave the church as enthusiastically as they had entered it.

But at the seminary, once that first mass was over, people mingled and welcomed back the students they had met the previous year, while also getting to know the new arrivals. As they left, they waved and shouted to us in French, "A la semaine prochaine!" (See you next week!) The experience was overpowering for me. Every day included attending a well-prepared celebration of mass, setting aside time to say the rosary, for meditation, private prayer, scriptural and spiritual reading; and all this interwoven in a day of study and community activities. The environment nourished me in a very rich, spiritual life.

Sunday evening, we had the last newcomers' conference, which was quite timely for me. The topic was particular friendships. To that point in my life, I don't think I had ever thought of any of my friends as particular friends. The message was that we were not to be friends with any one particular person, which meant not hanging around with the same person all the time for fear that others might feel excluded. Al, an American and someone I quickly befriended, looked over at me and smiled.

At the time, I was too naive to realize there was a lot more involved in the institute's concern about "friendliness" among the students; it was very closely related to my own concern about being attracted to males.

Not having any particular friends couldn't possibly make my life any more complicated than it already was, so I didn't worry about it. Al and I did study together on a regular basis. That was partly because even though we both had French backgrounds, neither of us commonly spoke French, nor had we ever studied in French.

The French culture was in my blood and I understood my parents when they spoke French, but growing up in an English community in Ontario, I had spoken English at every opportunity. Al, an Acadian, had been raised in Boston and had had a similar experience.

We found ourselves being taught in French, but English was our first language and we were both used to and more comfortable with English.

Life at the seminary was full of fraternal teasing and joking around. Everyone, at some point, became the subject of someone else's prank. Despite my childhood having lacked affection and affirmation, the one gift that my parents, especially Mom, gave to all of us was a sense of humour. My brother and sisters and I still have this innate ability to see humour almost anywhere, and to laugh at almost anything. That ability was as much a Godsend at the seminary as it had been at home.

One weekend, which had been designated as an outing for everyone to visit Quebec City or Montreal, a few of us who had a natural connection to each other through all being rather loud, flamboyant and always laughing, decided to do something on our own. Our plan was to steal (no other way of saying it) a gallon of sacramental wine from the kitchen cooler and sneak down behind the seminary to a cabin that was used for small team meetings and as retreat space. Since no one was on retreat that weekend, we used the cabin as our outing destination.

But the plan had three flaws. First, none of us had ever drank a full glass of sacramental wine which has a high alcohol content.

Secondly, though we had gotten through a glass each without feeling any pain (actually we were in pretty good spirits), we hadn't anticipated what it would be like after four or five glasses.

I, in particular, had a very low tolerance for sacramental wine — and a complete loss of mobility after four glasses.

By late evening when we decided it was time to return to the fold — the supply of wine having been depleted — we agreed that the one among us who could still walk on his own would be the forward lookout, moving strategically ahead, securing the way for the two who were helping me navigate, and keep quiet in the process. Thus, we continued back to the seminary, up the stairs and down the corridors to our rooms. If we met anyone, the plan was to say that we'd had a good evening out, which was, we convinced ourselves, only a partial and small lie. Luckily, no one else was about at that hour.

Spending most of the rest of the night "hollering" into the porcelain telephone gave me painful pause enough to become aware of the third flaw of the adventure, and major lesson of the evening, which had to do with just how sick someone could get on sacramental wine.

By the following morning, word had gotten out, thanks to my colleagues in crime, that I was very ill. Our team leader, surprisingly not too concerned about the over imbibing, felt compelled to remind me of the dangers of particular friendships. Meanwhile, he, being from Sri Lanka, had frequently enjoyed being with other students from that part of the world. The rest of us had accepted that as natural, yet he saw our little group as a clique. His apparent jealousy bothered me because each of us had been going out of our way to be friendly with everyone. But at the same time, I must admit, the sense of fraternity I felt with others in our little group was more than community; it felt like family.

Shortly after arriving at the seminary, we had each been asked to choose a spiritual director from among the priests, someone who would be our personal mentor and confessor, with whom we would meet monthly, or more often if needed. I chose an elderly priest who was a professional graphologist and had long ago studied this science intently for three years before counselling others based on an analysis of their handwriting. He and his art fascinated me.

With hindsight, he had been the perfect choice for me. He was a kind, forgiving and patient father image. He helped me understand what was being asked of me through the spirituality of the institute. He knew through analysis of my handwriting what I wasn't saying, yet he just listened, encouraged and respected my silence and my secret.

I remember telling him of my surprise at everyone at the seminary hugging each other when we returned from holidays and how, at home, I had never been hugged like that, not even by my mother.

After speaking to him about my attraction to and love of the woods, he explained, "Ray, as an introvert, nature and the woods will always rejuvenate you because it's in them that you feel God's presence accepting you as you are."

I immediately thought of my secret and felt that he too, was probably aware of it. Along with God's presence in the woods, this man was part of my process of self-evaluation because he understood where I was coming from and was able to listen and counsel without judgment.

International students had never seen Canada's famous white stuff before. The branches of the spruce trees that first winter bent with the weight of their new covering of snow. The busy winter months passed quickly and even before the first signs of spring, seminarians from Quebec got quite excited at the prospect of preparing the maple trees and looking forward to maple syrup time.

Being French, I identified with their excitement as I recalled how many years before, Mom had introduced us to this sweet delicacy. She'd get several cans of maple syrup from the area in Quebec where she had grown up. While she had been born in Maine, she moved with her family to Quebec as a child. From her, I knew what the final product was like, but had no idea about the process that produced it.

We soon found out what the old wooden shack in the woods was used for. Inside was a massive drum in the middle of the room, and a vent in the ceiling. We needed to tap the trees to collect the sap — forty gallons of sap to make one gallon of syrup. But you couldn't walk off the ploughed trails without snowshoes, which most of us had never used before, and even with them on, we sank down several inches. So, not only did we have to drill holes in each tree and place a tap and bucket for the sap to drip into, but we had to do it wearing snowshoes.

I loved the fraternity and camaraderie of the whole process. Everyone's laughing at each other for either not drilling deep enough into a tree, drilling on the wrong side, or falling and finding it difficult to get back up in snowshoes all made the labour more like play.

Once started, the process required a lot of attention so the next few months were very busy. Many of us used our recreation time to maintain the wood supply needed for the fire under the drum, which we kept filling with sap. On sunny days, the warmth of the sun would cause the sap to drip more quickly so the trees needed more attention.

When the maple syrup was ready, it was poured through a funnel at the base of the drum into several bottles, which were for the kitchen staff, but some was poured in long thin strips onto a large pan filled with about two inches of patted snow in it. Then a popsicle stick was placed at the start of the strip and rolled, making a thick taffy popsicle; and what a treat it was!

We also broke eggs into boiling syrup and then scooped them up and poured syrup over pancakes and desserts. It was a most anticipated time of the year and quite a treat for all of us, especially for those from other countries.

Just before my second summer at the seminary, my parish priest arranged for me to work as an orderly at the Catholic hospital in my home town. Getting VIP treatment and skipping the normal employment channels of working for a few weeks or a month at a time at different vineyards and fruit orchards in southern Ontario left me very grateful. My mother was ecstatic to have me nearby!

I enjoyed the job, though giving a sponge bath to a young, well-endowed man proved a bit awkward. He got an erection while I was washing his genital area. He sheepishly apologized as his face reddened considerably.

"It happens," was all I could say, but I was thinking, "Thank you, I'm flattered."

Though he was definitely more uncomfortable than me, it was the first time I had ever been in the presence of a man with a hard-on. I wondered why it had happened to him in particular and quickly realized the whole incident would have to remain our secret.

Being an orderly offered me the opportunity to experience myself as a compassionate person. Many of the patients just wanted to be heard. I was uncomfortable not knowing what to say to them, but always managed a smile and wished them well. I felt comfortable in that environment and was soon sent to different parts of the hospital to help out.

One day, the administrator asked me if I would be willing to work in the morgue with Dr. Brown. Without a second thought, I accepted and was soon talking to Dr. Brown.

"Ray," he asked right off the bat, "have you ever seen a deceased person before?"

"At a distance," I answered.

"So why did you accept this job?"

"I thought it would be a great opportunity to see the makeup of the human body firsthand... and to understand why and how autopsies are done."

He raised an eyebrow, but just said he needed someone to assist him for the next few weeks because his regular assistant was on a leave of absence.

"When do I start?" I asked with enthusiasm.

"Now," he said giving me a very quick tour of his department before handing me an apron.

"Put the cap and gloves on as well." He walked toward a covered body on a steel table in the middle of the room. Then, with one hand holding the edge of the white sheet covering the body, he paused and asked, "Are you ready?"

"What will happen if I faint?" I creased my brows together.

"I'll leave you there until I'm finished."

I told him I was ready. He removed the sheet, revealing a man's naked body. I expected an odor but it was minimized, by keeping the room quite cool.

Dr. Brown handed me the end of a rubber hose that led into a very large glass container and asked me to follow the scalpel with the open end of the hose, which would suction up any liquid as he began an incision.

The experience was almost unreal. Rather than wanting to faint, I was mesmerized as he opened the ribcage wide, exposing all the organs. I was in absolute awe, fixated on the organs, the colours, how compact and neatly fitted everything was.

At each step in verifying the cause of death, Dr. Brown explained what he was looking for. If an organ was discoloured, for example, that would lead to his looking for something else. Then we took the organs and weighed them, including the brain. I was amazed at the myriad of details involved. Then he sewed up the body.

Throughout the whole process, Dr. Brown was as respectful of the deceased as any of his loved ones might ever hope.

When I got home that day and told my parents about my pro-motion to the morgue, Mom said, "You call that a promotion," and we all had a good laugh.

The hospital experience made me feel alive, a part of something and less lonely, the activity and variety of tasks excited and invigo-rated me.

Interludes

My studies during the first three years at minor seminary focused on philosophy and a wide range of thinkers from Aquinas to Voltaire. We studied the Scriptures line by line. As future priests, we needed a thorough grounding in the Fathers of the Church, from Alexander the Great to Vincent of Lerins.

Then there were the studies of the seven sacraments, the seven deadly sins, the Ten Commandments, the doctrines and regulations that came from Vatican Councils; added to all that were the studies of moral ethics, Latin, the study of Jesus (Christology), of Mary (Mariology), of church history (ecclesiology), and basic psychology.

I was completely immersed in these studies, on a kind of auto-pilot. Christmas, Easter and the summer holidays came and went, the end of this phase of my life was fast approaching. All I needed to do was to continue studying, doing the 5-5-5, continue being accepted and, before realizing it, the priesthood and all it would involve would be upon me. With that thought, I felt more and more like a part of me was being cut away, sacrificed, that a part of me didn't belong. The old feeling of being alone resurfaced.

On each visit home, my parents met me at the terminal where my habitual hug for Mom was habitually not reciprocated, and I simply shook Dad's hand. Initially, we'd all be happy and excited about seeing each other again, and the first evening would be spent catching up with news about the family, distant relatives and the neighbours. However, my mother was soon at me with relentless persistence.

"Ray, call these people, they have been asking about you and they'd really like to see you."

In hindsight, I believe my reluctance to fall into the role she expected of me came from my soul's yearning to be fully and honestly myself, to shed the secret and damn the consequences. I didn't completely understand that at the time, so it's no wonder she didn't. Mom just returned my reticence with a look of disap-pointment and further insistence. It was always about her.

"Every time I see them they ask about you and say they're praying for you," she'd say. "If they knew you were home and didn't call them, what would I say to them?"

She'd look at me in her own certain way and trigger the same emotions I'd had before ever leaving for the seminary. My reluctance to visit everyone on her list increased with each visit and she confronted me every time.

"Ray, I don't know why you bother coming home, every time you come back, you're worse."

What she wanted was for me to reflect well on her and make a good impression in the community as a seminarian. This always left me in disbelief and hurt.

As for Dad, in his loyalty and devotion to the church, he would have made a great crusader, not that I would have been proud of him for it. My studies included church history, the popes and the crusades. I tried to share these with him, but he always insisted, "The church must've been right in what it did because the Pope was doing the Will of God."

Even relationships with my old friends changed. They wanted to hear about my studies but couldn't understand how I could choose a life without women — and I was unable to tell them I simply couldn't see myself having a life with a woman.

My first Christmas visit home did have its positive side. The priests were expecting me at church for weekday morning mass at 8:30 a.m. the day after my arrival. After mass, they invited me to serve at the upcoming Christmas midnight mass and the three masses on Christmas Day so they could introduce me to parishioners. When I returned home with this news, Mom was beside herself with glee. I was struck with disbelief myself at being handed the Christmas Midnight Mass and the three Masses on Christmas Day!

Most of the time, however, I was torn between the excitement of wanting to be home to share my experiences, and the conflicts I seemed to create by being there. With each visit, Mom seemed to find me more independent and opinionated, which she didn't much like. I was fighting to become my own person, but her expectations of me as a seminarian dominated my time at home. Invariably, I fought back tears on the bus ride back to the seminary.

With all my internal conflict after completing minor seminary, I wasn't eager to immediately continue with the remaining four years of studies in theology. Instead, those old thoughts of pursuing monasticism kept coming to the surface. To find some clarity, I discussed the options with my spiritual director, who listened attentively. I told him the prospect of continuing my studies right then made me feel caught, very alone, and scared.

"And I don't really know why," I said.

"Ray, follow your heart," he responded compassionately, "and be open that God may call you back here, and I will support your decision."

So, plans were made for me to spend the summer at Our Lady of the Genesee Monastery in Geneseo, New York. I'd experience the Trappist community during the summer before returning to the major seminary — if God didn't call me to be a monk in the meantime.

I flew home to meet my family, who then drove me to Rochester, New York, and on to Geneseo, which rambles through rolling valleys that stretch as far as the eye can see. The landscape is patched with cattle ranges and thick forested areas that give shade to the livestock. It was a beautiful, though very long drive on that day in 1967. We were beginning to fear we were on the wrong road when suddenly, there it was, the monastery stood about a half mile off the main road.

We were met by a monk who asked us to go to the residence on the other side of the road, which was a beautiful building that dated back to the American Civil War era — a plantation in its own right — surrounded by massive weeping willows. We had arrived at the guesthouse.

A few monks shared their time with us, showing my family and I the property, my guest room and the monastery gift shop, which sold Monks' Bread, their main source of income. My parents' purchases of it, along with other items made by the monks, especially cheese and chocolates, generously supported the enterprise. When it was time to say goodbye to my family, the look of disbelief in my brother's eyes that I was actually going to stay in this place was unmistakable.

"It's so quiet," he kept saying.

My mother, though she seemed to appreciate the silence, shared his sense of disbelief at what I was embarking upon.

That evening after their departure, the soft breeze and the warmth of the day were the perfect incentive for a stroll by a large fishpond situated beyond the guesthouse among some magnificent, huge willows. My sense of peace and connection was immediate, but I wasn't there long when the silence was broken by a strong male voice.

"May I join you?" he asked. My name is Henri Nouwen... and yours?"

"I'm Ray... Buteau," I replied hesitatingly.

Henri Nouwen was a writer visiting the monastery for the first time, apparently to work on a manuscript. At the time, I think I must have been the only seminarian who didn't know who he was. While we were there together, he offered me the opportunity to read excerpts from his manuscript, *Cry for Mercy*.

Henri took an interest in who I was, in my background and my studies. We enjoyed the evening under the willows, and did so on many subsequent, wonderful occasions. We had lengthy talks on spirituality or just chatting casually as friends.

He returned in 1971 and stayed for seven months while he wrote the Genesee Diary. But while our paths and life experiences crossed again over the years, we never met again.

Thirty-one years later, I studied the writings, especially his book *Wounded Healer*, and learned again the importance of just being present to others.

And forty years later, I discovered that Henri and I had been living the same spiritual struggle and pain of being alone in not having been able, as priests, to live out our lives with a significant other. I eventually learned that we also shared the same secret, and that we were not the only two priests with that secret.

My first day at the monastery was as surreal as my first day had been at the seminary years before. Even though the monks were not to have idle chatter among themselves, I picked up on a strong sense of fraternity among them and quickly learned that charity toward monks within a monastery is to respect their need for silence.

They gathered in the chapel seven times a day for prayer — The Divine Office (liturgy of the hours) was recited in Gregorian Latin chant. The lights were always dimmed when they entered the church and made their profound bow of adoration to the altar and cross, and then moved silently to their stalls to pray, sitting, kneeling, or squatting on their heels in their large, tan-coloured garments with the big hoods, which dated back to the twelfth century.

The atmosphere of silence and prayerfulness within the natural setting of the monastery, encircled as it was by rolling hills and miles of trails through beautiful forests, comforted me a great deal. Wallowing in the profound spiritual experience, I found myself losing track of time.

The Voluntas Dei Institute had its 5-5-5 and the monks had their 8-8-8: eight hours of prayer, eight hours of work, and eight hours of sleep. They considered their work to be part of their recreation in that work offered a lot of exercise.

While working or during other regular activities, interactions at the monastery were never distracted by idle chatter or indiscreet questions or comments; we just accepted each other's presence. The simplicity of the lifestyle struck me — no one had unnecessary possessions or nic nacs, which kept their living spaces, and their minds, uncluttered. Like the woods, they too, accepted my presence in silence.

I was well accepted by the community of monks and there was an interest in my returning, but I hadn't realized at the time that there was a minimum age requirement of 25 years. I was just 23. The monks suggested that in the interim, I could apply for a position with a Catholic organization (The Techo Foundation), a branch of the American Peace Corps that would require a two-year commitment from me.

They suggested that more life experience would help me decide if I really wanted to enter their order when I turned 25.

While still at the monastery, all the arrangements were made for me to enter The Techo Foundation (Spanish for roof/shelter). My parents were surprised that I would be accepted based only on my mother's American citizenship and even more surprised at my willingness to go ahead with the plan rather than return to my studies.

The contact priest for the Techo Foundation met me in Manhattan and drove me to Briarcliff Manor in Ossining, N.Y., a very exclusive part of the upper city. He said the mansion I would be staying at had been part of the Rockefeller Estate. We drove up to a high stone fence with a large, decorative, black metal gate that opened to a circular drive in front of the three-storey, medieval-looking castle. With a smile, he said, "Welcome to your new home, Ray."

"*And what a magnificent home it must have been,*" I thought as we entered the lobby, with its regal spiral staircase. My companion priest wished me well and led me to an office to sign a two-year contract. I had to take an oath of secrecy stating that any pertinent information whatever that might be, would be given to the director only.

We were 15 young adults studying Spanish and the culture of Chile, where we'd be sent. Men were on a separate floor from the women, and each floor was off limits to the other. My room met my needs: a comfortable bed, a desk, recliner, and a large window overlooking a forested area, which comforted me as I settled in.

We met in the lounge for orientation and a tour of the mansion. It included a classroom, a lounge, library, dining area and a massive ballroom that was used for charity events. We'd host events to support our project in Chile.

In the lounge, we introduced ourselves and told the others how we'd found out about Techo... and to hear about how this sole Canadian had gotten in. What we had most in common was our idealism, good intentions and a keen interest in volunteering our services in another country.

We were given a study timetable, books and tapes to study Spanish and reference material on Chile. Our church services were at one of two nearby institutions: Kings College, which has since burned down and been relocated and the Maryknoll Missionary Centre for priests preparing for work in Asian countries.

After only two weeks in the program, because of the political situation in Chile, our project there was suspended. Instability in the country eventually led to a bloody coup in September, 1973, ending Chile's democratic government and installing the ruthless dictator Augusto Pinochet.

We had a new project: working in small second-hand clothing stores in the Bronx to gather information about tenement housing in the area and report our findings to the director.

Working at the store was nothing like I had ever experienced. I'd never met gypsies and knew nothing about their European origins or cultural characteristics. They looked a lot like street people to me, and they had what I thought was a Slavic accent. I was told they were great at bartering and loved to argue pricing, so I was warned that it was important not to get upset, and to gain their respect by at least trying to barter with them. I spotted my first gypsy by her attire as she piled up three boxes full of clothing. Having been fore-warned, I wondered what to charge for each article. She had other intentions. Sizing up this naive 23-year-old, she called me over.

"I give you good business," she began. "I pay for two boxes and you give me one box free."

I paused to do my own sizing up, and then replied, "I'll make you a deal... you pay for these two boxes, and if you don't want to pay for this last box, you can leave it here until you can pay for it."

With that, she launched into a raging verbal attack, ending with, "I'll tell my friends that you're not a good person!" She left the three boxes, and me, looking bewildered. One of the other workers came up to me smiling.

"You'll see her here tomorrow," he warned, and sure enough, she was back the next day. At first, I was a bit apprehensive, fearing a conflict but she merely stepped up and paid for all three boxes.

When we weren't working, we were given money and day passes to downtown New York City. Yes, the Big Apple! I was young, adventurous and very naïve. After the sightseeing tours and walking in Times Square, I caught sight of all the magazines being sold from a small street corner newsstand. I soon spotted one with three young men in bathing suits standing very close together.

"May I see that magazine?" my hands were sweating in my pockets.

"Are you over eighteen?" the attendant narrowed his eyes at me.

"Yes," came my meek reply to the question, which seemed rather odd at the time.

As I opened the magazine, my heart pounded as I stared at men having sex with each other. Other pictures immediately conjured fantasies in my mind.

After what must have seemed like a lot of gasping on my part, he asked, "Are you going to buy it or hand it back?"

"I'll take it," I said with downcast eyes.

With a huge, knowing smile, he asked, "Would you like me to put it in a bag?"

"Yes... please," I said. Throughout the magazine, I found the names of bookstores, bars and bath houses... whatever they were!

On my next day pass, I headed straight for Greenwich Village, which was a world of its own, and walked into my first gay bar. I drank my beer nervously, playing with the coaster while trying to look around as non-chalantly as possible. I was among others like myself, I knew that, but I was too shy and emotional to speak to anyone. I listened intently, absorbing how they spoke and behaved. While my anxiety was high, it all felt good, like I belonged. In spite of my insecurity and apprehension, that place felt comfortable to me in a way that I struggled to understand.

Oddly, I was reminded of how, as a teen, we would ride our bikes from St. Catharine's to Niagara Falls. Along the way we would stop by the orchards and help ourselves to some of the fruit from the trees along the road. The farmers wouldn't mind as long as we didn't take a basketful with us. There was no harm in picking a large, ripe red Mackintosh from a big apple tree and savouring that first, particularly juicy bite of forbidden fruit – something off limits, yet strongly desired.

My next visit to the village in search of another bath house took me through neighbourhoods and down side streets that I was too naïve to know could have been dangerous. The address was right, but there was no sign indicating a name, only a red light above a door. I followed two men in and, once inside, found another door in front of us. To our left, a man sat at a counter behind a cage-like screen.

"Room or locker," he asked the two ahead of me. They asked for a room.

"And you?" he asked me, barely bothering to look up.

"The same," I said, not knowing any different. I paid and he handed me a key and towel and buzzed me into the lobby.

"Could you tell me where to find this room? This is my first time here," I said.

A man standing nearby said he would show me the way. Favours don't come without a price, and they certainly didn't in that place.

The hallways were very dark. Once inside my room, I locked the door behind me. While taking off my clothes, I could hear moans and groans even through the loud background music.

WARRIOR OF THE RAINBOW

There was a locker for all my belongings. With only a towel on and a key on a wrist band, I was ready to leave the room.

Other men stared at me, some smiling and others nodding their heads. Not knowing how to respond, I kept walking around, passing opened doors to rooms with men lying on beds, some with, and others without their towels on. I smiled, too naïve to know better.

Finally, I found a place to sit and watch how others behaved, trying to understand how they were communicating and acting. A very good-looking man about ten years older than me introduced himself.

"This is my first time in a place like this," I admitted the obvious with a nervous quiver in my voice.

He probably thought, *"Lucky me!"*

"Would you like me to show you the place?" he asked.

Again, too naïve to know better, I nodded.

He showed me all the back rooms and explained the subtleties of eye and body language. He seemed to want to befriend me and spend time talking. He offered me a drink and we went to the lounge to sit and watch the porn video that was playing. Sitting close to him and watching porn was quite arousing for both of us. He had years of experience over me and had his own intentions in taking me under his wing. I learned a great deal that day, including some valuable lessons about the games people play to get what they want. He got what he wanted and, after the apple was bitten, I was no longer a virgin.

It wasn't the way I had imagined it would be in my fantasies with Steve McQueen. Caught up in the erotic sexual high energy of the place, I hadn't been prepared for the kind of intense encounter in which I felt I was about to pass out.

Afterwards, my partner seemed kind and caring toward me, wanting to buy me another drink and continue chatting to get to know me better. But my only thought was to escape from what had become my new reality, and from the new awareness of how naïve and alone I was. Not only had there never been anyone with whom to share my secret, but there was also no one I could talk to about my first sexual encounter.

I fretted over how I was ever to meet others like me in Canada. Were there even any magazines like the one I'd found in New York? For the moment, I took solace in knowing that in the broader world at least, I was not alone, and could enjoy New York while I was there.

Working in the second-hand clothing store was generally pretty quiet, aside from having to be on your toes with the gypsies. That was, until the day three burly black cops came charging in telling us to lock up and drive as quickly as possible out of the Bronx. As whites our lives were in particularly perilous danger in that black neighbourhood on that day.

"If anyone tries to stop your car just keep driving," one of them said.

"But why, what's going on?" someone asked.

"Do as you're told; you could be killed if you stay here!" came the loud response from an impatient officer.

We got the message and within seconds everyone's adrenaline was at full throttle as we ran for the car and went speeding through the neighbourhood getting to the highway as quickly as possible.

In that black community, pedestrians who caught sight of us waved their fists at us, but we drove too quickly to react, speeding through stop signs and red lights as safely as we could.

Once on the throughway, someone finally had the presence of mind to turn on the radio. Martin Luther King Junior had just been assassinated! Back within the safety of the centre, my heart was still pounding, until we were given a debriefing by the staff.

It was April 4 — my mother's birthday — so I called home. "Happy Birthday Mom," I said when she picked up the phone, and then quickly moved on. "Have you heard what happened?"

Like a large part of the world that day, Mom was in a state of disbelief. I told her about the excitement of my day and how it wouldn't be safe to return to the store at all. As it turned out, that store was destroyed by angry neighbours and we had to be assigned to another project. We had a few days to process the reality of what we'd been part of — though far from the site of the actual assassination, we had been among the people for whom Martin Luther King Jr. had had a dream.

My personal experiences in The Big Apple helped to connect me to that part of myself I had felt I had been cutting away at minor seminary. That was good, but I had problems with the organization. I'd signed up for a project in Chile, not two years in the Bronx under an oath of secrecy that I was not comfortable with at all. Now there'd be another assignment to another used clothing store and more secrecy. I'd had enough. Despite the director reminding me that I signed a two-year contract and leaving meant I couldn't apply for another project with any American agency, I quit. I was done.

It was 1968 and I was only 24 years old. I couldn't return to the monastery, and I was cutting my ties with The Techo Foundation, so, to Mom's relief, I decided to continue my studies and enter major seminary back home.

Major Seminary

The decision to return to my studies and get back into the spirituality of the institute felt right, though I was certainly not as innocent as I had been when I left. Knowing there were others like me also felt good.

A seminarian met me in Perth Andover, New Brunswick, to drive me to the Institute Voluntas Dei major seminary in Red Rapids, N.B. As we drove, we were encircled by rolling hills, narrow roads with rock cliffs bordering them, and forests that seemed endless. Periodically, a farmyard appeared next to large fields of red soil.

After travelling half an hour through the rolling countryside, to my right, at the top of a high hill, the two-story, long brick buildings that formed the major seminary campus came into view. As we took my luggage to my room, I began meeting friends who were now a year ahead of me after my sabbatical in New York. Classes would begin in a few days so I had time to settle in and re-orient myself. The priests were young, and one in particular was very good-looking.

As in minor seminary, most of the seminarians were international students. The mix of nations in our team, the cleaning chores, visits to the merchants for food supplies, the 5-5-5, the team meetings, the fraternity, the evaluations, were all familiar to me. But there were differences. We were told, for example, that first-year students would form a parish team and assist a priest from the seminary in serving several families in the immediate area who attended our Sunday services. The other seminarians were also divided into parish teams with priests from the seminary assisting the parishes and missions in the diocese in more general ways.

We would be giving children and adults religious instruction, preparing them for the Sacraments of Initiation (first communion, first confession and confirmation) and to be altar servers. The teens formed a youth group with their own activities and socials. And along with leading the congregation in singing, we'd greet everyone as they entered and left the church. We would also have opportunities to visit families and shut-ins.

As it unfolded, team meetings were often attended by the priest who was part of our parish team and our spiritual director. The meetings gave each of us the opportunity to share our reactions and concerns about the experiences we were having, not only at the seminary, but also in the parish setting. We experienced the positive aspects of parish ministry, including the respect and gratitude of the people.

Unfortunately, it was a false indication of how we would often be treated as parish priests in later years because we were not exposed to the administration and politics within a parish community and a diocese. I was naïve to think that entering major seminary would really give me a better idea of what the priesthood is about.

Our studies in scripture, sacramental preparation, dogma and ethics were more intense than they had been in minor seminary.

Besides our practical pastoral experience, we were given courses in public speaking, homiletics, and catechetical teaching. There was a sense of serious preparation for ordination in just a few years.

The studies about God and the Roman Catholic Church had often seemed to me like a process of dissecting an animal and studying every organ. I would regularly ask myself if a relationship with God was really that complicated. This was not a hospital morgue, after all. Would the process lead me to feeling any closer to God? Closer than I felt just soaking up the natural beauty of the area, with its panoramic sea of colour in the fall, the red soil of the fields in spring; the congested growth of green potato plants ready for harvest by late summer?

For me, God was easily accessible in the breathtaking autumn scenery with the maple trees revealing the best of their reds, oranges, yellows and browns as far as the eye could see in any direction. By mid-fall the walking trails were rivers of crackling, ankle deep leaves still sporting their splendid colours. Being a part of it all was, indeed, a spiritual experience.

In winter, the spruce trees were weighed down with a thick covering of fluffy, powdery, sparkling snow. The paths were kept clear for walking and in the evening when the moon reflected off the snow, you could clearly see into the depth of woods and the small river running through them. Being a part of it all was, indeed, a spiritual experience.

In contrast, during our studies, frequent reference was made to us as being another Christ, to being the representatives of Jesus on earth, leaders and models of church authority. We were "in the world but not of the world." That notion made me feel somewhat separate from the parishioners, being made to believe that I was somehow closer to God as his servant and representative on earth than they were. In nature, I felt his presence in a way that comforted me much more than theological ideals and catchy slogans.

Before entering my fourth year at major seminary, my soul nagged me constantly: "*Are you ready to deal with adults and their life issues and concerns, let alone a generation of young people searching for truth and independence?"*

My mind would not rest: *"And your secret, how are you going to deal with it 'in the world but not of the world'? You're different from those around you, Ray."*

My soul was anxious about my not being "of the world" if that meant somehow leaving the world that had others in it like me, though I was not connected with any of them at the time. I spoke with my spiritual director about gaining more clarity about my future through more pastoral experience before resuming the formal, academic journey toward ordination. I suspect I was having last minute cold feet about becoming an ordained priest and taking my secret into that world, but he supported the idea and I was off to Manitoba.

I was granted permission to stay at the bishop's residence in St. Boniface until I could find my own lodgings. My hosts had already been informed of my having successfully completed my third year of theology, of not having been attached to any diocese, and looking for pastoral experience. They greeted me as a potential candidate, especially since I was bilingual in French-speaking St. Boniface.

Soon after finding work as an outreach worker at a Senior Citizens' Centre, the bishop asked, "Ray, would you be willing to do weekend pastoral work in one of our parishes?"

I said yes and thanked him.

"You'll be assigned to Blessed Sacrament Parish, a facility that serves two parishes, one Catholic and the other Anglican," he said.

It was my first experience with this kind of ecumenism and gave me the opportunity to meet many families from both communities, some of whom remained my friends for many years.

The folks at the seniors' centre were mostly of Ukrainian and Polish background. They were a proud people with strong traditions and heritage. The elderly ladies treated me like a grandchild, spoiling me with baking and beautifully crafted gifts. They were also knowledgeable about life and insightful from years of experience. They reminded me of my dad because they often appreciated someone taking the time to listen to them. That was all part of the up-side of the experience.

However, also like Dad, many were often biased and self-righteous. A discussion could often turn into a heated argument with anyone who thought differently, which was uncomfortable. But then, once again like Dad, by the next day, all was forgotten.

It was during that time in Winnipeg that I was introduced to Omer at a gathering of Oblate missionary priests. I had occasionally expressed an interest in working with aboriginal people and Omer had heard about it.

"Ray," he asked me, "would you be willing to make a commitment to working for me for two and a half years up north? It's in a community called Repulse Bay."

He explained that it was on the Arctic Circle and the people there refer to themselves as Inuit. With a smile he told me, "I'm the Bishop of the Arctic."

I agreed to go and he told me to be ready in three days.

Omer was pleased, but Mom? Not so much! When I called her with my news, all she could say was, "Oh no, Ray! The Arctic?"

Not a Tree in Sight

Three days later, all I could see out the window of the plane for endless, mesmerizing miles was a terrain of white and grey with patches of blue. Finally, a break in the scenery came when I caught sight of a large herd of caribou running at full speed, as if being chased. The plane turned, descended sharply and a village appeared along a shoreline. I could see no roads leading in or out of the community. *"This place is in the middle of nowhere,"* I thought.

As we touched down on a narrow gravel airstrip, I could see several Mongolian-like faces with all sorts of expressions I didn't know how to interpret. Everyone was in parkas with fur-trimmed hoods of various colours. Mothers carried small children in large hooded attachments on their backs; all were anticipating the arrival of the plane and the Kabloonas — the whites from the south.

I was with a people who were very child-like but far from childish. They took delight in teasing, being spontaneous and carefree. If I was being tested by them it was so I could survive among them, not merely to achieve a passing or failing grade. To get annoyed or angry is a sign of weakness and rejection among the Inuit. Similarly, to accept the teasing and laugh at oneself are signs of strength and acceptance.

In the south, people often feel used by others, but in the Arctic, everyone is needed. In the south, people often tell others how much they love them, but in the Arctic, I could see that people were shown they were loved — words were not needed. It was wonderful not having to perform well to be accepted; I just had to be.

I felt as if I were watching a movie, not knowing what the next scene would bring, but knowing I'd be in it. Events happened quickly, unexpectedly, with no time between takes. Scene followed scene and I played my part, trying my best to follow the script. Whether digging through five feet of ice to fish, waiting motionless to spear a seal alongside a hole in the ice, laying traps for foxes and rabbits, or shooting ptarmigans, caribou, and polar bears, the days and weeks spent on the ice were full of activity.

The Inuit had accepted my presence among them, and that I had learned to survive and live among them, no more, no less. No trophies were offered for valour or courage. Eventually, when I was preparing for my return south, my friend who had invited me in for tea and had led the hunt and given me my Inuit name, asked me why I was leaving. I could only speak from my head, not my heart.

"I have to," I said.

In my heart, I knew that in spite of a positive experience in the community, I couldn't remain a single man there indefinitely, living like any normal person, and also be myself. Nor could I become a priest and be assured that I would return to this community, and even if I did, the isolation and not ever being among others like me would have been too difficult. So, all my concerns went into that simple response: "I have to."

I wiped tears from my eyes as I boarded the plane. As we ascended, the community disappeared quickly from view, but to this day I can visualize every person and every corner of the community. And though there were no trees, I still felt God's presence in the incredible beauty of the natural world and the varied wildlife.

I experienced a way of life that even then was rapidly disappearing. Climate change, social influences from the south, government policy, and a generation of Inuit losing touch with their culture have altered the Arctic forever. We've all seen films and talked to people who've been where that dotted line called the Arctic circle crosses the map of Canada. But most of us don't know the people or their land. I was blessed to know both.

Ordination

Upon my return to Winnipeg in August, a local priest approached and asked me to help him out. "I've just been made principal of a junior high school," he said, "and wondered if you would be interested in teaching religious studies to grade 7-9 students."

"That's in just a few weeks!" was my startled reply, but I accepted the offer, grateful because it would give me the opportunity to work with youth before ordination. I knew I'd have trouble defending certain teachings of the church that I wasn't too comfortable with myself and, sure enough, at one of the first classes, a student asked, "If God is unconditional love, why would he condemn us to hell for missing mass on Sunday?"

"Couldn't agree more with you," I thought to myself, but replied, "I understand... but the church teaches that it's a mortal sin to miss mass on Sunday."

It was an inadequate and transparent answer that was met with indifference and a hesitant smile.

Not long after getting re-settled in the city, the Chancellor of St. Boniface asked if I would consider being ordained for the Diocese of St. Boniface. He wanted to be supportive but he also wanted to keep me in the province.

"Thanks," I said, "but I'm rather uncomfortable with the tension between the English and French in this diocese."

"If you'd like to meet with the Archbishop of Winnipeg to discuss the matter, let me arrange a meeting with him," he replied.

I knew he had my interest at heart, so I agreed. The archbishop at the time was Cardinal Flahiff, a distinguished-looking man with a gentle, humble presence. After hearing about my studies and pastoral experiences, he thanked me for coming and invited me to come back in a few days for more discussion. When I returned, he wasted no time getting to it.

"Ray," he said, "would you consider taking a year of studies at St. Augustine's in Toronto? It's affiliated with the University of Toronto where you'll be taking some of your theology classes."

He explained that he felt it was important for me to take my last year of theology in English to become familiar with English terminology in scripture and better prepare me for presentation and celebration of the sacraments.

"Consider it," he didn't press me for an immediate response. "If you're in agreement, come back in a few days to fill out the forms and we'll make preparations for your stay at St. Augustine's."

I found my connection with nature while in Winnipeg at either the Assiniboine or St. Vital Park. It was in Assiniboine Park near the city zoo that I walked long and pondered hard this latest development. The background sound of some of the zoo's resident exotic birds blended with the local varieties while a gentle breeze only slightly disturbed the leaves of the giant oak and elm trees towering above me.

"*What a change.*" I thought as I recalled the contrasting, tree-less, yet equally spiritual Arctic terrain.

While enjoying the peace and tranquility of the park, one question kept coming to mind: *"Had my studies at Voluntas Dei and my pastoral experiences been to prepare me, not only to go to the seminary in Ontario that I initially didn't want to attend, but also to become a diocesan priest, which I had also avoided?"*

I had no feeling of regret about not returning to the Voluntas Dei Institute in Quebec. A lot had happened since I finished my studies there; I'd moved on. I felt gratitude for the wonderful memories and experiences the institute had given me. In fact, I felt surprisingly good about the cardinal's offer and decided to phone home with my decision.

In those years, every time I phoned home, Mom held her breath, hoping I'd have news of plans to complete my studies and settle down. So when I called and said, "Mom, I've decided to return home," she responded as she had over the previous few years.

"Oh Ray," followed by a long, negative sigh.

"I don't mean I'm moving back home," I quickly added. "I mean I've been accepted to the Archdiocese of Winnipeg and Bishop Flahiff, is sending me to St. Augustine's in Toronto for my last year of studies."

"Oh Ray," she repeated, with a lot more energy... "Wait till our parish priest hears about this."

St. Augustine's is a large institutional-looking, brown brick and stone building, distinguished by a massive cross atop a dome. The entranceway is huge, with a high, pillared approach to the doors. Entering for the first time felt rather surreal to me, knowing all our previous parish priests and bishops had walked through the same entranceway as young men.

Inside, the wood-panelled walls, marbled floors, wide hallways, high ceilings, and a chapel that was larger than our whole church at home were impressive, indeed. Our individual rooms were larger than my apartment in Winnipeg had been.

While I was moving in, some of my neighbours dropped by to introduce themselves and welcome me; I quickly made a new group of friends. One of them later became the bishop of my home town. The dean eventually became Archbishop of Toronto and later a cardinal.

Canon Law, the church's regulation in regards to the sacraments, was among my studies that year. A course in liberation theology proved to be a major influence in my life because it made me aware of clergy struggles in different parts of the world — priests who struggled to support the needs of their people — and the church hierarchy that didn't want priests involved in politics. I found it to be the most insightful course in revealing similarities and parallels with the need for justice that gay priests had themselves been facing.

We took classes in how to celebrate the various liturgies and in leading a community in worship. In practising to say mass, attention was given to posture, movement, gesture, articulation and reverence. We practised hearing confession, conducting a funeral and administering the sacrament of the sick, often referred to as last rites. I found the classes practical as well as visually and creatively appealing.

Some seminarians were preparing to be priests in my home town. Others had the young priest who'd spent a summer teaching me Latin as their bishop.

At the time, I thought I was still the only one with the "secret" and was constantly asking God to help me repress my feelings. Yet, years later, a sexual scandal made the news about all the homosexual activity that had been going on at St. Augustine's Seminary at the same time I was there. I was shocked because I hadn't been aware of it, nor had anyone ever spoken of it. What hurt me most was all the anguish I had put myself through thinking I was the only seminarian who'd had the thoughts and feelings I did. I was naively living in the midst of others who were, obviously, just like me.

After St. Augustine's, I returned to Manitoba. My year of preparation for being ordained as a deacon, the last step before final ordination into the priesthood, took place in a Winnipeg parish. It was similar to the one I had spent time at in 1971, serving a Catholic and an Anglican community.

One day, when my bishop was visiting, he came face to face with the Anglican priest, who excused himself for not knowing how to properly address a cardinal. My bishop extended his hand and said, "I was baptised, George." I was impressed that despite his rank, he was able to maintain humility and humour.

As a child, I'd been taught that the Catholic Church was the only true church, and wondered if those who taught and preached that actually believed it themselves. Working closely with other denominations marked the beginning of my questioning of our differences, whether they were important or relevant, and if God really cared about such trivial distractions. The Anglicans I met were as devout, spiritual, faithful and Christian as any Catholic.

I was Catholic only because I'd been born into a Catholic family. I had always seen all religious groups and faiths as no better and no worse than any other. Everyone had different beliefs and rituals, but all had a love of God. I had always been aware that we, as Catholics, were different, but I never felt that we were better, somehow holier or more pleasing to God.

The pastor of the parish was a pleasant young priest but his live-in housekeeper made her position clear.

"If you want anything in the kitchen, let me know," she said bluntly upon my arrival.

In other words, it might have been my home, but it was her kitchen, and she had a presence about her that forcefully said, "Don't cross me!"

At the time, the Manitoba Department of Education asked me to update its Arctic collection by working with graphic designers and scriptwriters to produce a slide documentary for elementary students. Entitled *Inuit – the people of Canada's Arctic*, it's still available through the department.

I lived in two different worlds, one of parish ministry and the other of document preparation. The latter offered me a distraction and diversion from parish appointments and meetings, which I appreciated as a cause outside of parish ministry. It was as if I needed one foot outside at all times in order not to leave an important part of myself completely behind.

As my ordination approached, the pastor called me into his office. His usually pleasant face was lined with worry, "Ray, I want you to keep in confidence what I'm about to tell you."

What he said next shocked me.

"I won't be able to attend your ordination. I'm leaving the parish in a month. I've asked to leave the priesthood because I'm engaged to be married."

He gave me a moment to catch my breath and continued. "I'm sorry to be telling you all this as you begin your ministry."

Oddly enough, I felt really happy that he had the courage to move on in his life by embracing freedom and love. He was a kind and gentle person, and God had given him the greatest gift, the love of another, though others may not have expressed it that way. It certainly was an interesting way to begin my ministry — and prophetic!

As a deacon, I had the opportunity to get a better idea of what the priesthood was all about. I was assigned to a neighbouring parish set in a wooded area along the Assiniboine River close to Assiniboine Park, a perfect setting for me as I prepared for ordination into the priesthood. The pastor there was only too happy to give me all the pastoral experience I needed as a deacon, in preparation for being on my own as a priest in a few months. He asked me to attend all parish meetings: administrative, liturgical, catechetical, social and outreach.

Presiding over baptisms, weddings and funerals that didn't have a mass included preparing three to five meetings with couples before their wedding or having a child baptized. Meetings with the family were held before a funeral for spiritual support and to help arrange the service according to any specific requests, which had to conform to diocesan regulations. Conducting the wake service before the funeral came next, then presiding at the funeral itself, and the interment, attending the reception, and then follow-up support of the family a few days later.

Funerals were quite involved, powerful, spiritual experiences for everyone involved, including me. As the saying goes, it's not over till the paperwork is done, so certificates and registry information had to be filled in and appropriately filed.

As for weddings, many couples were not comfortable with everything the church, through me, was asking of them. Besides all the preparation classes, they were encouraged to attend church more regularly and to have their children raised in the Catholic faith. Many merely went through the motions.

Even before becoming a priest, though I enjoyed meeting the couples involved, I found myself becoming demanding about them abiding the church's rules. I even took their indifference and lack of enthusiasm personally. I had heard priests talk with cynicism and an air of self-righteousness about these "pick-and-choose" Catholics, and I seemed to be developing into one of them.

"Hi Mom, it's Ray..." I paused and, in anticipation, she said nothing.

"I have the date for my ordination."

"Oh, Ray," she said with excitement and, I think, some disbelief.

I told her it would be May 19, 1978, at St. Paul the Apostle Church in Winnipeg.

When the day came, my family and an uncle were present, along with many priests, who were there to show their support and fraternity. A group of young people with lively and uplifting voices and the music of guitars, flutes, tambourines, and a keyboard offered powerful energy and emotion that accompanied a beautiful religious celebration led by Cardinal Flahiff.

My family was impressed and relieved I was finally a priest. They'd been waiting 14 years. Like a wedding, I only had to say,

"I do" but, unlike a wedding, I went to bed alone that night. I'd fantasized about a few men in the parish but I avoided succumbing to the desire to be more than friendly for fear of being discovered and outed.

2

RESPECT

Parish Ministry

My first assignment as an ordained priest was assistant pastor at St. Augustine of Canterbury Church in Brandon. Although the pastor was well-liked and respected locally, somehow my relationship with him immediately took on tones reminiscent of the relationship I had with my mother — getting along was a challenge.

Early on he was anxious for me to do something with the youth in his parish as soon as I arrived in the city. A young nun who was also just starting out in religious life was anxious to speak to me. She was a delightful, energetic person with a cause. She wanted to introduce me to a program for teens called "Search." Her enthusiasm and conviction kept my attention and the more she spoke about it the more interested I became.

It was a highly active program, a live-in weekend retreat involving the teens and three couples who'd act as chaperones and be involved in a number of other activities. A great deal of planning, preparation and, of course, money were needed, but the Sister knew how successfully the program had already been implemented. With manuals detailing every activity, a list of talks prepared and financial needs laid out, we agreed to meet again to plan a strategy. Every step was accompanied by prayer.

In time, with a detailed outline of the program in hand, we met with the pastor to ask for permission to present the program to the parish committee, which included the finance committee.

Unfortunately, the pastor didn't share our excitement but said he would pass the idea on to the bishop for approval. He made it very clear that it was his parish and any project would only take place with his input and blessing.

Word spread that we were planning a live-in teen retreat. Calls started coming in and we lay low waiting for Sunday when we knew the pastor would get blasted with questions from parishioners. On Monday he called me into his office and gave the project his blessing.

Sixty participants attended our first Search weekend. It was such a success that we had a waiting list for another one. I was attracted by the free spirit of the young people, their vitality, energy and openness. Some saw themselves as committed even though they didn't attend Sunday services on a weekly basis. They'd follow in their parents' footsteps when the need for the rites of passage came along.

They knew that if they didn't attend religious studies they would not get "done" and were apprehensive about what the emotional consequences of that might be. In response, some acted out, withdrew, and became aloof, sarcastic or overly opinionated. They had to conform to fit in and be accepted and that frustrated them immensely. I could relate!

Though I found one young man in his early 30s in our Search group sexually appealing, I could never fathom the idea of seducing him, nor any other man that appealed to me because I still believed I was the only Catholic male living with the fantasies that I had.

Ministerial meetings of all the Christian clergy and leaders of other faiths, a new experience in my personal ministry, were held monthly in Brandon to discuss issues of social and moral concern in the community, and to see if, as a faith community, we could have input in supporting charities and social agencies. We also sought to be supportive of one another as faith leaders. Many maintained a respectful distance and were reserved while among their colleagues.

I found an important fraternity and support in ministerial groups but it wasn't long before I saw the different denominations and

Christian groups, of which there are several hundred, as independent business groups that were protective and self-righteous about their beliefs and their requirements for membership. The Catholic Church — from my perspective — was certainly among them, no worse and no better than any of the others.

My friend Jim, a young, charismatic, energetic and open-minded evangelical minister, was visiting one day when he said he had to leave to get ready for his ministerial meeting.

"What do you mean, your ministerial meeting?" I asked with surprise, knowing he attended the same ministerial meetings that I did and I knew nothing of a scheduled meeting that day.

"The evangelical ministers have their own ministerial group," he replied.

"Are you telling me there are two Christian ministerial groups in this city?" I continued in disbelief.

"Yes, this meeting is for Christian ministers who can publicly say they accept Jesus Christ as their personal Lord and Saviour."

"And you believe the rest of us can't?" I asked. "No one ever asked me."

I was dismayed that this sort of thing actually existed, which only emphasized the rift that already existed among Christian churches.

"So," I went on, "if I were to publicly say to your group that I accept Jesus Christ as my personal Lord and Saviour, I could join?"

Jim looked at me with a wide smile, realizing I was game to do it, and said, "I don't see why not."

"Good," I blurted. "I'm going to change and I'll go with you… Are you alright with that?"

"This will be interesting," he responded.

"If you don't mind picking me up so I don't have to walk in alone?" I added.

"My pleasure," he said. "I'll pick you up in half an hour."

Thirty minutes later, I walked out in my black, three-piece suit with Roman collar and cuffed sleeves.

Jim laughed as I got into his car. "I can't wait to see their faces," he said.

We walked into a group of about a dozen men and women who, when they looked at me, went completely stoic. Most of them already knew me from the mainstream ministerial. We took our places around the table and the chairperson acknowledged my presence. Thanking him, I bluntly broke the ice.

"I'm aware that to be present in this group I need to acknowledge my acceptance of Jesus Christ as my personal Lord and Saviour, which I do."

The immediate tension and ill ease in the room was palpable.

"Thank you for your declaration," the chairperson responded while the others sat stunned and obviously annoyed.

After the meeting, during hot coffee and a cool reception from one and all, I told Jim, "If we can't have respect and acceptance among ourselves, it's a good indication that the process of healing the divisions within the Christian faith has a long way to go to reach what was said of Jesus' followers: 'See how they love one another.'"

He nodded in agreement.

The wave I created that day was no tsunami, but perhaps it was challenging enough for a good surf.

In Brandon, I was often rejuvenated by God's presence at a nearby park where I was almost instantly calmed, comforted and strengthened. Many of the friends I met in those early days after my ordination remained a part of my entire priesthood. I became part of their family fabric and they came to know a great deal about me — except my secret with God. Yet, out of my loneliness and insecurity, I had tremendous trouble in Brandon, particularly with the pastor.

I had managed to keep my anger with him pent-up inside for two years before it came to a head one day as I was putting on my vestments to say mass. The pastor came up to me and sternly complained, "Ray make sure no lights are left on after mass."

"Now, he's treating me like the caretaker," I thought.

But before I could even suggest the church caretaker take care of such things, he continued.

"And make sure the doors are all locked as well."

Then he stood, staring at me, waiting for some sign that I would obediently comply.

I wanted to let it go and just tell him his timing was terrible, that this was not the time to discuss trivial matters, or anything at all. I needed to prepare myself for mass in just a few minutes, but he didn't seem to care. He regularly intruded into my space and I was always intimidated and afraid of confrontation. This was my first assignment as an ordained priest and he was my superior. What was I to do?

Well, this time something snapped! It was like he had thrown a lit match on gasoline. I lost my ability to think rationally. "Damn!" I said under my breath, glaring at him with all the intensity and resentment I could muster. If looks could kill, I would have slain the man that very moment. I found myself breaking through that wall between us.

Livid, I stripped off my mass vestments and flung them at him as he stood and stared back at me in shock.

"You have a mass to say!" he yelled. "What are you doing?"

"No!" I fired back, barely able to control my anger and trembling body. "You have a mass to say! I'm out of here!" I turned and wanted to run right through the door.

"The bishop will be in touch with you!" I told him as I slammed the door behind me.

I gathered some personal items in the rectory and drove to Winnipeg. I must have stopped for gas at least, but all I can remember of that drive is the dividing line on the highway.

A few years previous, friends in Winnipeg had told me that if I ever needed help to call on them. As I crossed the Perimeter Highway into the city, that invitation played in my mind like it had just been offered.

It was late evening when Jake opened the front door of his house to see me standing there like a stray cat, suitcase in hand. His face told me he could sense that something was very wrong the instant he lay eyes on me.

"Ray?" he said tentatively, as I slowly entered and he took my coat. "You wanna go downstairs and rest?"

"Thanks Jake," my throat tightened and my eyes watered.

"Is there someone I should call?"

I told him to call Father Dominique.

We went downstairs and I parked myself on the couch in his basement family room. Jake and Wanda had lived in the same house for several years with their son, Chris. It was a modest four-bedroom bungalow in the St. James area of west Winnipeg. Along with a living room, dining room and kitchen on the main floor, there was a fully furnished basement that served as a recreation area with a TV, ping-pong and pool tables, and a small bedroom for visitors and drop-ins like myself. A two-car garage was attached to the home.

"The bedding and towels in the bathroom are all clean," Jake said. "I'll leave you to it... we can talk in the morning."

I said nothing. It all seemed so surreal. I was in a state of disbelief as I moved about like some kind of zombie, getting the bedding out, undressing and trying to make myself comfortable on the couch. I was dead tired and should have been able to sleep on a bed of nails, but as I replayed the scene with the pastor over and over, my anxiety grew into gut-wrenching fear, of what I wasn't sure, but sleep eluded me.

After a fitful night, I got up early showered, got dressed and went upstairs to find Father Dominique sitting at the kitchen table with the family.

"Morning Ray... how are you?" he asked, obvious concern in his voice.

"Scared," I sat down next to him as he poured me a cup of coffee. "I don't know what to do. I feel like hiding somewhere for awhile."

Chris had been listening from across the table. "Father Ray, you could stay with some of my friends," he said.

His parents turned to him in disbelief.

"Chris, Father Ray is not one of your hippie friends," Jake said.

"How do think your friends will feel about a depressed priest staying with them?" I asked him. And as the words came out of my own mouth, I felt the tears welling up in my eyes. I wanted to scream and cry and simply disappear in the utter hopelessness that I'd ever find someone to share the aching hurt of my loneliness and frustration.

"I'll just tell them you're a friend who needs a place to stay, a guy who needs to be left alone for awhile," he replied confidently, his mouth full of Cheerios. "And if you pay for your room and board, they won't ask questions."

"Sounds like you have some nice friends," I said, taking another sip of comforting hot coffee.

"They're just a group of people who decided to move in together to support each other in taking care of the house they rent. It's not a four-star hotel; they'd probably give you the spare room in the basement with nothing but a mattress on the floor."

I thanked Chris and decided to give it a shot. I had to stay somewhere. Jake offered the basement family room for as long as I needed it, but we all seemed to know instinctively that I'd be more comfortable at arm's length from close acquaintances. I asked Chris if he'd take me over to meet his friends.

After breakfast, we all talked a short while longer, then Jake and Wanda left for work before Chris took me to his friends' house, a huge rambling, three-story near the Assiniboine River in the

Wolseley area. I was taken downstairs and shown my room, which, as Chris had warned, consisted of a closet, a mattress on the floor and a small window high on the south wall. Thankfully, Chris's parents had supplied me with bedding, towels and blankets.

I met a few more of the young tenants in the kitchen of the big house, but I don't remember any of their faces nor, for that matter, the food they offered me, nor any other details about the house. The clearest memories I have of my few weeks on that mattress are of my bedside companion — the house cat — and how exhausted and emotional I felt the whole time.

Father Dominique had been a well-respected Oblate Father who was also a trained psychologist. He was retired, and as an old friend was more than willing to visit me daily. He gave me paper and a pen to journal with, and on subsequent visits he'd listen to me share my written ramblings. I wrote often, long and furiously; it flowed out of me as if from a bursting dam.

Father Dominique told me he'd support my taking time away from the parish and would assure the bishop, Cardinal Flahiff, that I was safe and would appreciate money for room and board to support my hosts. Later, he told me the cardinal wanted to assure me of his prayers and best wishes.

I got up whenever I awoke, but spent most of my days in my dark little room sleeping, crying or writing. My daily prayer, which I would say several times, went like this: "Dear God, I don't know what has happened to me or how long this will last, but I know that you are caring for me and that I will be okay."

One evening toward the end of my stay in Wolseley, I was out for a walk when I suddenly became very frightened that I might meet someone on the street, anyone! I had never experienced anything like that before and, sure enough, I soon spotted someone coming towards me and was filled with anxiety. I quickly crossed the street to avoid him and got back home without actually coming face to face with anyone. The whole experience made me aware of just how weak and vulnerable I had become.

Until that evening, I had always enjoyed the streets in the area. Many of them are thickly lined on both sides with large elm trees, their branches reach over the sidewalks to touch each other in the middle, forming a protective green canopy over the street and the people below.

After the fearful walk, I was exhausted and needed sleep. Without invitation, the cat curled up next to my head and we closed our eyes. This quickly became a part of our routine any time I lay down to rest.

A few days later, as I awoke from one such escape from reality, with my furry friend very near my head, my gaze was drawn to the small window. Outside, I could see the bright blue sky and for some reason, felt filled with a new energy, like a new person. It was as if I'd been in a deep coma for a long time. I looked around in dismay that I'd slept on that mattress on the floor for almost a month. I felt compelled to leave.

I got up and thanked those of my hosts who were present and said goodbye to the cat who had been my constant companion. He had literally been a godsend, a guardian for this human, a creature that could sense my dis-ease and instinctively give comfort, almost healing, with his intimate, undemanding presence. And, like most cats, when he sensed that I had been healed, he did as most cats do and ignored me.

Before my stay with Chris's friends, I'd never experienced young people who would offer such hospitality to a stranger, with no conditions, expectations or comment, other than a few words of gratitude for my financial support. I knew, as I left their home, that my time with them and their cat had been a spiritual experience. They were not, by any means, religious, but they had been very spiritual in their compassion and hospitality. I believed they found great favour with God and they hadn't needed to be religious to earn that favour. That was an epiphany for me.

I had asked Cardinal Flahiff for a transfer away from Brandon and, unknown to me, he had been approached by Sister Viola, a pioneer in ministry with the deaf, and totally committed. She'd asked the cardinal for a priest to help her offer pastoral care to the hundreds of families with a deaf member. Sometimes an entire family was deaf. She asked for an energetic and expressive priest that could help her develop a parish community — Church of Silence. Guess who the cardinal had in mind?

"Ray," he said, "if you're willing to accept Sister Viola's request, you'll be sent to study at Gallaudet College in Washington D.C. and stay at Immaculate Conception Parish on Massachusetts Avenue. You'll earn your stay by helping out with their parish masses."

Excited about the proposal, I immediately asked, "When do I leave?"

"In a few days."

The last time I'd been told that I would be leaving in a few days, I found myself heading for the Arctic. This experience would be far from that, but once again, the idea of doing something outside the status quo, away from the unhappiness of my usual life, gave me a feeling of freedom and exhilaration.

The residence on Massachusetts Avenue was like a small estate, with five assistant priests, a cook, a housekeeper, a sacristan, and a care-taker. On the same property were an elementary school, a parish hall, and an administration building. The parish supported a few charities and a few less fortunate black parishes.

"Welcome Ray," the pastor said with a wide smile upon my arrival. "I suggest you get to sleep early since starting tomorrow morning you'll be saying the 6 a.m. weekday masses."

Of course, mass at 6 a.m. marked the beginning of my day — well before breakfast. I was quite surprised to see over 100 people at each mass, along with a choir of five well-paid professional singers. For the most part, the attendees were professional people starting their day with prayer.

Typically, when I returned to the residence for breakfast before heading to the university, I entered a long dining room with priests scattered around a huge table reading their papers and eating their breakfasts. Once in awhile someone would comment on what they were reading, otherwise they read and ate silently except for a local radio channel playing in the background.

After breakfast, I took a standing-room-only bus to the university, surrounded by men in three-piece suits in the heat of summer, standing there looking comfortable while I was sweating in a short-sleeved shirt.

"What deodorant are these guys using?" I often wondered.

After getting off the bus at Dupont Circle, I caught the subway to campus. During the regular school year, several thousand students at the college used sign language. I arrived as one of a few thousand summer students, a beginner, who could communicate only in English. Once again, as when I was among the Inuit, I felt isolated and disconnected, but accepted. The contrast to my Brandon experience was not lost on me. Everyone was so expressive I could often piece together what they were talking about by their body language and facial expressions.

I managed to get through the beginner and intermediate programs in the three months I spent in Washington. My stay was a privileged experience that offered me insight into a very wealthy class of people who often used their gifts and resources to help many people.

Having touched the edge of the world of those in power and influence in Washington, and the world of those who lived in silence at the college, this was an important part of my spiritual journey.

But then the call came from Winnipeg and I never got the opportunity to use sign language again.

"Ray, this is the bishop; I need you to return to Winnipeg as soon as possible," he said with a sense of urgency.

"Father Ted has had a severe heart attack and needs immediate attention and rest... you're the only priest we have available to replace him."

"I'm sorry to hear that," I told him. "I'll make immediate arrangements."

In the priesthood, changes often came quickly and it was my duty to be available and ready. My personal preferences were secondary to the needs of the church.

With only a few hours before my late-night flight, I found a counter with a variety of take-out food. I purchased an exotic drink, a large deli sandwich loaded with everything, a decadent dessert and looked for a table. Outside, near a ramp to a car park, I saw a small manicured piece of lawn with a few small willows and a picnic table. I headed outside, dodging other travellers and on-coming traffic. I claimed the picnic table and spread out my bounty.

With traffic steadily passing by and people walking up and down the ramp nearby, God's presence filled me with absolute bliss. I had two hours to enjoy the grass, the blue sky and the gently swaying willows before heading to my boarding gate.

With my banquet before me and nature's magnificence around me, with the backdrop of a busy international airport, I was very aware of how God's presence could be experienced, though not always easily, in the midst of anything. While savouring every morsel of food, sip of my drink and the warm breeze, I gave thanks to God. Full of hope, I was ready for Canada and a new experience of parish ministry in a place called Winnipegosis, Manitoba.

I was in cattle country almost immediately after crossing the north Perimeter Highway beyond the Winnipeg city limits, heading north. What else could you do with land that's dotted with marshes, huge rocks, and minerally-challenged soil? An hour had passed and, except for the occasional field of grain or sunflowers, the scenery hadn't changed. I passed small villages that were well out of sight behind me within the count of ten. The farther I travelled into the land of the moose, elk, and bear, the more road kill I saw on the highway and its shoulders.

Approaching three hours out of the city, I came upon the fair-sized community Dauphin, with lots of stores and more than one gas station. But half an hour later, I was again travelling down a corridor of highway lined with fir trees until a large lake appeared, Lake Winnipegosis, which was so large I couldn't see the other side.

Then, out of nowhere, appeared the Village of Winnipegosis, where I was to be pastor of five communities composed primarily of people of Polish background. I was reminded of my days at the seniors' centre in Winnipeg. Many Ukrainians and Mennonites also lived in the village, and a number of aboriginal communities were nearby. Most of the people were descendants of hard-working settlers, strong in their cultures and traditions. Change was difficult for them.

The Catholic Church, which held about 200 people, was well kept, in large part because of the efforts of the local church ladies' group and six Benedictine Sisters, who also ran the community hospital. The Sisters played the organ on Sundays, led the choir, supported the ladies' group and knew everyone in town. Before long, I became extremely grateful for their support and friendship. Their main religious community and retreat house were just north of Winnipeg and became like a second home for me. I always felt welcome there, as did anyone else seeking a retreat.

Interwoven into almost all aspects of the community, the Sisters were often my source of sanity and encouragement. I was also very grateful to their cook, who was constantly baking and preparing beautiful meals; I jumped at every invitation to partake. They also had a huge garden, which I not only benefited from as a source of fresh produce, but also as a place of solace.

Church services were always well-attended and parishioners were uncommonly active in catechism programs that we introduced for their children. Parish and finance committees were set up in each community and ladies groups raised money from annual fall suppers, rummage and bake sales.

Parishioners kept my freezer full. The men supplied me with all kinds of wild meat, duck and fish; the women kept me full of pastries, deserts and other goodies, as well as homemade dinners.

Winnipegosis was a commercial fishing community, which gave me the opportunity once a week to go out on a fishing boat and net my fill of pickerel. We'd leave at 4 a.m. and return at 4 p.m.

Sometimes the boats would get close to each other and the language at times would be rather crude. The men on my boat enjoyed warning those on the other boat.

"You should be careful of your language; we have your pastor on board."

Of course, their own language wasn't much better and everyone had a good laugh.

My second parish, in Pine River, was farther to the northwest and a half-hour drive through a thick, forested area that seasonally attracted hunters from far and wide looking for moose, black bear and elk.

The people of Pine River took great pride in their homes and properties. The ladies' group was well-organized and the craft and bake sales were crowd pleasers. I recall one elderly lady who was losing her sight, yet she made hand-crocheted tablecloths that were really fine art. In larger centres, they could have been sold as such, full of precise detail, the culmination of hours of loving work over several months.

When I left the community, she gave me one of her tablecloths as a gift, which I will never part with. It represented what she couldn't say to me in words, like the care packages that Mom mailed to me at Christmas.

The ladies kept the parish viable and were friends and a support for each other through times of joy and difficulty. They were an amazing group of women.

Ethelbert, another of my parishes, was half an hour's drive west of Winnipegosis. If you were not Polish in this community you were considered an outsider, and the priest was no exception. Perhaps it was a good thing that being an outsider was not new to me.

The parish was run by two families that were related and entrenched in Polish customs and religiosity. The church was small and rustic, holding about 100 people. A wood stove was situated in the middle of the aisle. The three altar boys were in their late teens, as tall as me and quite hilarious. My organist, Dan, was a young Ukrainian friend of theirs and the four of them kept me sane with their youthful antics. I met Dan again in October, 2000, at his world premiere musical, *The Strike*, about the 1919 Winnipeg general strike.

The little church was full and the people were dressed in their finest at my first Easter service in Ethelbert. A Polish elder, who was the church patriarch, was smiling at me before the service, I guessed, to make sure we were on good terms. As we prepared for the service in the sacristy just off the main sanctuary, the altar servers decided to hand me a letter saying that they were going on strike for higher pay.

"I don't give you guys anything," I told them in disbelief.

"That's our point," one said. "We'd like some of what you will receive today."

Knowing that I'd probably get a few dollars as gifts, I agreed. But they knew something I didn't, which, of course, was the basis of their whole hidden agenda.

Just before the service, the patriarch came into the sacristy to tell me that Jesus was lying in front of the altar.

"Who is lying in front of the altar?" I asked, bewildered.

One of the altar servers spoke up to tell me a statue of Jesus lying in the tomb was always placed in front of the altar before Easter mass. I had to go and wave the incense smoke over it, sprinkle it with holy water, and say a few words, after which they would say "Amen" and we'd return to the sacristy. So out we went, and sure enough, there it was. I did my thing, and we returned.

The patriarch came back and asked me to wait for a few minutes. The altar servers were smiling a lot.

"Jesus is now on the altar," the patriarch said upon his return, then quickly returned to the sanctuary.

"He was dead a minute ago and now he's on the altar?"

I asked the servers, who could hardly contain themselves. "They took the dead Jesus out and put a statue of the resurrected Jesus on the altar," one explained.

I did my thing again, they said "Amen" and we returned to the sacristy.

"Are there any more statues?" I asked.

"No," one of them said, "but you're going to have to look at the back side of that one for the next forty days."

Finally, the mass began and everything was going along well until the collection. The patriarch marched towards me carrying the collection basket and handed it to me.

"Why are you giving this to me?" I quietly asked him with a forced smile.

"It's our custom," he told me. "At Easter, you have to pass the first collection."

I looked at the servers.

"It's the custom," Peter repeated with a shrug.

The whole congregation was looking bewildered that I didn't know what was going on. I got up with my basket in hand and Dan played the organ like a pro. I went from pew to pew, smiling and thanking everyone as they put money into the collection plate. It took me a few minutes to manoeuvre with my vestments on but, finally, it was over and I sat down while the ushers took the second collection.

After mass, the patriarch came back to the sacristy to tell me they would need a few minutes to prepare things. I looked at the servers, and asked, "What things?"

"They're going to get some Easter baskets of food for you to bless," one said, "then we go back out and sprinkle water on a few of them."

They knew very well that when we went back into the sanctuary everyone in the church would have a huge basket full of food. I thought I could bless the crowd with one symbolic sprinkling for all, but no, the custom was for every one of them to come up to have their basket individually blessed with holy water. Where they were getting all the holy water I dared not ask.

Finally, back in the sacristy I thought it was over when the patriarch came again, thanked me and ceremoniously handed me the collection I had personally taken.

"This is for you," he said with a smile of satisfaction.

"What do you mean, for me?" I repeated in disbelief.

"It's our custom that the first collection at Easter is for the priest and his needs."

I thanked him and he left, then the servers approached me with wide anxious smiles.

"A deal's a deal," they chorused. "And without us you would have been lost," one added, not realizing the larger truth of his words because those boys were truly a comfort to me.

One year, word got out that it would be nice to have a large Christmas tree in the church in Winnipegosis. A few weeks before Christmas, one of my young friends came over to tell me he and some friends had just put up a tree in the church and I should go see it. Indeed, a huge tall tree stood to the side of the altar at the front of the church. It was massive and perfectly shaped.

"Where did you get it?" I asked in amazement.

"A donation," he said. That same day, the police came over to ask me if anyone had spoken to me about a tree that had been cut down and taken in the night from a Ukrainian woman's property.

"No," I answered truthfully. "No one has come to speak to me about that."

There were a lot of suspicious looks in church the following Sunday morning — at both the tree and at me.

"An anonymous donation," was all I could say.

After one of the church services in Pine River, a quite short, elderly man wearing a suit that was likely in fashion in some much earlier era, asked to speak with me. People seemed happy to see him, though he rarely came to church and was rarely seen in the village.

"Do you have time to come over to my home today?" he asked.

I told him I did.

"What are you driving?" he asked.

"A Ford, LTD, four-by-four half ton," I replied.

"Good, follow me," he said.

I had no idea where we were going as we drove north out of the village. Several miles later, without a crossing road or driveway anywhere in sight, he turned his signal light on and headed for a ditch.

"*Where is he going?*" I muttered to myself. As I slowed down to follow him off the road, tire tracks could be seen leading into the woods. Tree branches hit my truck as we went farther and farther into the bush. Finally, we came to a beautiful clearing.

"Wow! I don't believe this!" I said. In front of me was an authentic log cabin with a rustic front porch. Beside the cabin was a large enclosed corral with horses, cows, pigs, sheep, goats, chickens, geese, and a mule. It looked like the roundup for Noah's Ark, but no large boat was in sight. A little farther to the west was another corral with double log-rail fencing that sagged between rotting posts.

The entire homestead was situated at the edge of a very large valley. Across the valley I could see high hills, or what I came to know as Manitoba mountains. It was autumn and the panoramic view of the valley and the hills beyond in all their brilliant colours was truly spectacular.

We got out of our vehicles and the old guy invited me into the cabin. There was no electricity, so he lit a lamp. I felt like I had stepped into another era. The cabin consisted of one large room, a few small windows, wooden shelves, a wooden table and chairs, a cot, and clothes on pegs at strategic spots on the walls. Piles and piles of well-thumbed *National Geographic* magazines, lay everywhere. There was no toilet in sight so I knew where it likely was.

"May I give you something to drink?" he asked.

"Yes, thank you," I said.

As he took a white cup from a hook on the wall, passed a cloth over it, removed the lid of a 45-gallon drum and submerged the cup into it, I quickly asked, "A drink of what?"

As soon as he took the lid off the drum, the smell of pine needles was almost overwhelming. He just smiled slightly as he handed me the cup. I was about to have my first full cup of pine-needle wine and I knew that it would have a very high alcohol content. One sip and I was in trouble. I nursed it along very slowly, like champagne, but champagne it was not.

The old man was very kind and gentle, soft-spoken, and he appeared to be in good health. He reminded me of my father in many ways. My father would have thought he was in heaven had he seen the cabin and its idyllic setting, and he would have liked this old gentleman.

"How long have you lived here?" I asked him.

"Sixty years," he replied.

As we sipped our wine, he explained that he'd begun to settle the property in his twenties. He was married but his wife died shortly after and he never remarried. He never mentioned children and I didn't ask. He said he knew of a few other men who lived like he did, as hermits. Some had since died and, he said, he would soon join them.

"What do you mean?" I asked.

"That's why I asked you to come here, Father. I want to tell you what I'm about to do, and would like to ask you to deliver this letter when I'm gone."

He handed me an envelope. "As a priest," he said, "I know that I can trust you, and I would like you to do this for me."

"How can I help?" I asked.

"We know when we're about to die," he continued.

"After we've settled our affairs, we go into those hills you see on the other side of the valley... and go into a cave that we have prepared for ourselves. We enclose ourselves and wait for our last breath."

In silence, we sipped the last of our wine.

"In a month," he continued, "if the people in the village haven't heard from me, give this letter to the police. Tell them that I entrusted it to you... no more than that."

I nodded in agreement.

In a matter-of-fact tone, as if he were talking about the weather, he said, "I will give my animals away before I leave. I believe in God and I know that He will care for me. I've had a good life and have been very happy here... but it's time for my life here to end."

Feeling privileged to be in his trust, yet sad knowing that this would be the only time we'd see each other, I listened to him share parts of his life story as we finished our drinks.

Afterward, we wished each other God's peace and I left him.

Two months later, a parishioner told me that people were looking for the old man. I immediately took his letter to the police.

That humble man had been living a very spiritual life with his God; there was no doubt in my mind about that. He hadn't asked for the last rites or for me to hear his confession, nor had I offered them. As far as I was concerned, this man didn't need them. He had been living in heaven and would continue to do so.

While in Winnipegosis, I befriended the Mennonite minister and we maintained contact for many years. Dan was an enthusiastic, young married man with a family. He had a strong faith and love of life. He spoke to everyone in the community no matter what denomination they were, and he was respected and loved by his Mennonite community, and by my Catholic one as well.

Dan was always very supportive of young parishioners who wanted to attend Bible college. He said that many young people, after attending Bible College, became more involved in their parish communities and some had considered parish ministries and even ordination.

"How odd that someone would be willing to take a year or two after high school to study the Bible," I thought.

Bible studies had been a Protestant concept to me since child-hood, when we were discouraged from reading the Bible at home. What a great leap to the current generation that wondered why the Catholic Church didn't have Bible colleges. Even the young people in the Search program in Brandon had often asked, "Why don't Catholics have Bible Colleges like our non-Catholic friends do?"

I got some insight into what they would experience at a Bible College from our Search program, in which young people had opportunities to discuss scriptural passages, issues of moral and ethical concern for them and to prepare liturgical celebrations. They learned to work as a team and experience mutual support and encouragement. Being among their peers they studied and discussed their faith in a non-threatening environment. Search weekends had a profound impact on all who experienced them. I could see how extending that experience over a year or two in a college environ-ment could be life-altering for young people. For many Protestant students, such studies were a rite of passage.

So, when a Catholic workshop was offered in Winnipeg on the topic of scriptural studies, I was immediately drawn to it. Those in attendance were concerned that their children didn't have the same opportunity as non-Catholics to attend a Bible College. Since I had often spoken about the subject with Dan, the idea sparked a keen interest in me and I let it be known. That evening, a few of us met with the facilitator of the workshop.

While there had been a lot of interest, only those willing to make a commitment to meeting regularly were asked to meet after the workshop to pursue the notion of a Catholic Bible college. Five committed souls remained late into the evening, and we decided to meet again in two weeks. We took each other's names and phone numbers and agreed to reflect on our personal interest and commitment after receiving feedback from others about the concept, and on questions and concerns for future discussion.

"Wait till Dan hears about this," I thought. I had been asked if I'd be willing to speak to the cardinal about what had come out of the workshop and get his reactions before we went any further. I would share his feedback at our next meeting. I called the cardinal right away and asked, "May I meet with you before returning to my parish concerning the workshop on scriptural studies?"

The cardinal, having been a scriptural scholar himself, welcomed my visit.

After telling him about our intended future meeting and the questions we'd be discussing, he agreed to meet with me again after our follow-up session. He seemed very happy about my enthusiasm and interest in the cause.

"May I have your blessing in pursuing this project?" I asked.

"Don't commit yourself without keeping me informed," he replied, and I returned to my parish.

The notion of scriptural studies became the topic of conversation with everyone I met in the parish. I gathered pages of input reflecting this considerable interest. The others in the group had similar experiences in their home communities and were equally well-prepared for a lively follow-up session. When we got together, we were all anxious to talk, and all at the same time, so someone had to chair the meeting and someone else had to take notes.

Out of that meeting, with representation from Saskatchewan and Manitoba, developed what we called the "Catholic Bible College Interim Steering Committee." I accepted the chairmanship, alongside a Benedictine Sister from Winnipeg as secretary, and we began formulating a concept vision, goals, priorities, and a meeting schedule.

"Before going any further, we need to prepare an outline I can present to the cardinal for his blessing," I reminded the group.

Then a member from the St. Boniface Diocese reminded us that the City of Winnipeg had two dioceses and would require the blessing of both bishops. Then it was noted that within the Province of Manitoba, there are five dioceses. How were we going to get representation from all of them? On whose behalf were we speaking? And on what authority and with what credibility did the committee consider forming a Catholic Bible College?

We had some political logistics to work out. We needed to be well-organized before discussing visions, concepts and all the related topics.

The cardinal informed us that a meeting of Western Canadian bishops was coming up and that he would like to notify them of what was being discussed and ask for their feedback.

We sat on our hands while they met. When the cardinal returned from the meeting, he reported cautious interest within certain guidelines.

The bishops suggested that a steering committee be made up of representatives from each of the Western provinces and from the bishops, priests and laity. The cardinal agreed to keep the bishops informed.

We were overwhelmed with this development because we hadn't yet really started discussing anything in detail. But we forged ahead and asked that the bishops from each of the Western provinces choose a bishop who would be interested in attending monthly meetings. We also asked the Council of Priests to choose a representative and provide representation from the laity. The steering committee would have a bishop, a priest, and at least two laypersons from each of the Western provinces and the Territories.

In addition, the cardinal could see that this would be a long-term project and would need administrative support, so he offered our secretary an office in the chancery, which also gave him a close eye on developments. Within the next month we had stationery, a phone, and were ready to do mailings and updates.

We were offered the facilities at the Grey Nun Centre in Edmonton, Alberta, for our monthly meetings. The executive knew the topics and issues that needed to be discussed and we organized our meetings to maximize the time we had and to exhaust the topics as thoroughly as possible, taking into account all the considerations brought up in previous discussions.

Our secretary drew up the minutes, sent out updates and made all the arrangements at the centre; all we had to do was show up on time. Each diocese made a great commitment in financially supporting our travel to Edmonton. The Sisters in Edmonton were great hosts and my own diocese was very supportive in offering the committee office space and a salary for our full-time secretary.

The months and years went by quickly. At the end of five years, the Bible College in Canmore, Alberta, opened. The vision had been to keep it a grassroots college, meaning that it would be run for and by the laity with continued support and input from the church hierarchy. But to have the church's continued blessing, it became top heavy with hierarchy and bureaucracy. Within a few years it closed! All the efforts that had been put into the realization of a Catholic Bible College evaporated.

At the time, I couldn't understand why the church hierarchy could let something like that happen when there had been so much interest and support. The closure had a profound effect on me. Everything had been going along so well. The laity especially, had spent years and many, many hours doing ground work, researching, reporting, studying with sub-committees throughout their provinces, meeting with bishops and finance committees, even finding a suitable building and hiring a director from applications received from across Canada.

The hierarchy had allowed the laity and the clergy to do all the work, but were determined to make it clear to everyone that it was in charge. Once the vision of a grassroots structure was lost, it all came apart.

Dan had not only been instrumental in my getting involved in the Bible college project, as frustrating and disappointing as it was in the end, but also in many of my more positive experiences in Winnipegosis. Early one evening, near the end of my time there, he came over to invite me out for supper. I found it odd that we were not having the meal with his family, especially since his wife had been so supportive of our friendship. I also found it odd that he was wearing a suit, which he only did for church services.

When we walked into the restaurant, no one else was there. He quickly said there was a buffet in the back hall but I immediately became suspicious. He opened the door to allow me to enter first and there before me was his entire parish community, standing at their tables and giving me a standing ovation. I couldn't hold back the tears.

They gave me a Catholic Bible signed by all of them. I will always cherish that gift, along with the many signs of caring and cherished memories of so many God-loving people in the Winnipegosis Parish.

After having worked on the Catholic Bible College so long and hard, I was left with my five small communities to serve, but no trips and meetings to plan, no cause to promote. A huge void and silence overtook me. I cried during the day but didn't know why. As the days passed, I felt extremely lonely, and yet there were so many friends and parishioners that I could have visited.

My spirit yearned for connection and for fulfillment as a gay male, for the sexual intimacy and companionship that the good people around me could never provide to a priest. I was trapped; a great part of my pain was in not being able to talk about my feelings, not being able to tell anyone my secret, which added to my isolation and loneliness. I needed a change.

I left Winnipegosis in 1985 to begin a new assignment in Dunrea and the surrounding four communities in southwestern Manitoba.

I was hopeful, but with that move, a growing perception of having undue expectations placed upon me only heightened. It started almost immediately with the men's Catholic organization known as the Knights of Columbus, along with the church ladies groups and a few pillars of the church, who were accustomed to befriending the priest and assisting him in running the parishes.

When I arrived, the task before me seemed overwhelming, especially when I realized that those who had been running everything really didn't want change while many others, including myself, did. The Knights were very active in all the parishes and were the main supporters of church activities and projects in the community. Since all the previous priests had been members of the Knights and I chose not to be, tension filled the air. They let me know that if I were a Knight, they were certain I would get much better cooperation and feel much more included.

It wasn't long before the bishop invited me to come see him. He wanted to know how things were going, though he already knew. After the usual fraternal hug and a friendly cup of coffee, he got to the point.

"I'm surprised to hear that you don't seem interested in being a member of the Knights," he pointed out all the good work the Knights do and the sense of fraternity and support the group could offer me. "Perhaps you should give it further consideration," he added.

As often happened at such cordial visits, little consideration was given to what I did or didn't want, which only served to heighten my isolation.

In Dunrea a few days later, the main Knight dropped over to see how I was doing. Within a few minutes the invitation to join was once again extended to me and I accepted, realizing I really had no choice if I wanted support in the community, which I needed. I felt I had sold my soul, and I had. I was caught between the expectations of the people and those of the bishop, with little support from either, and nowhere to turn.

Every parish had women who were seen as the pillars of the community. They prepared the children for the sacraments and when the children and their parents were prepared to be a part of the parish, the children received the sacraments. These pillars kept an eye on me to make sure I didn't move anything in the church or do anything without their opinion and permission. If I did, guess who they called?

Some families, who were not regular parishioners — seldom showing up at church or church functions — still wanted the rites of passage for their children. Some young couples wanted to get married in the church and yet were not actively practicing members of the parish. Parishioners would sometimes complain if I didn't hug all the children, or visit them as often as their previous pastor had done. I often found myself torn between the needs of those parishioners who were no longer attending regularly and the regulations of the church.

I was uncomfortable with many expectations and regulations of the church that many parishioners didn't want to follow, and which others couldn't follow, such as having to attend church regularly in order to avail themselves of its services. Mothers and grandmothers, for example, spoke of the pain of rejection by the church in not being allowed to have their children accepted for baptism unless they came to church more often.

But despite all the wrangling and criticism, the one constant enjoyable challenge were the meetings with young couples. I often saw myself in them, caught between the expectations of their parents and those of the priest. I secretly enjoyed their independent spirit; their seemingly rebellious outlook was refreshing, though I was often unable to provide them with the services they wanted without strings attached.

In preparing for marriage, they had often been pressured by their parents, and especially their grandparents, to get married in a Catholic Church. If left on their own, many couples would have been much happier with an outside, civil marriage, or for some, at least a hassle-free church wedding. Many parents and grandparents had an ingrained belief that unless one got married in a church, God wouldn't attend. With one in two marriages failing, every elderly Catholic grandmother was quick to explain why.

Couples wanting a church wedding knew what to do. They would show up for a few Sundays before asking to see me, making sure to greet me as they left the church. They'd agree to everything I asked of them, but the next time I saw them after the wedding would be when they had a newborn in their arms. And the cycle of getting the child "done" was passed on to a new generation.

In defense of these couples, they hadn't been given much of a choice. If they'd been honest about their intentions to simply use the church for a public ceremony, they would've been refused, been labeled by the institution as married outside the church, and therefore not in good standing and they'd have to live with that guilt trip.

If I could get them to at least consider the possibility of going along with church requirements, I'd give the green light to proceed, knowing that we'd likely go through it all again when they returned with a child in their arms.

I felt very alone, isolated and often at odds with the women pillars who faithfully followed the regulations of the church. I was immensely bothered by those regulations because of how annoyed people could get in having to arbitrarily conform to them, and because of the implication that somehow God was connected with it all — that by going along with all the regulations, one was doing the Will of God and by inference, by not going along, one was somehow disobeying God.

In my view, God didn't care one way or the other. They were church, man-made regulations, and the only people who really cared about them were those working for the institution, which, as a priest, included me. Subconsciously, and as time went on, not so subconsciously, that conflict took its toll on me.

To say I was not happy with parish ministry would have been a gross understatement. I couldn't see things getting any better, no matter where they put me. Yet, the majority of people were very kind and understanding so, at one level, I didn't understand why I was going through so much turmoil.

Why was I so unhappy? Why couldn't I settle down and stop taking things so much to heart? After all, as a parish priest, I had always lived a privileged lifestyle. My rent and food were always paid for and I had insurance, a pension and health benefits all under a diocesan plan. All my basic necessities were taken care of, the cost of which, for any of my parishioners, would take up the bulk of their wages.

In most of my parishes, someone else did my weekly house-cleaning, receptionist duties and property maintenance. My only financial concerns were my car payments; even my gasoline bills were partially covered. Outside of scheduled appointments, I enjoyed the freedom to go on personal errands and private endeavours without waiting for scheduled days off. There was no such thing as fifteen-minute breaks and half-hour lunches.

I had so much going for me: security, respect, independence, health and hundreds of supportive people that I could visit. And if I needed anything, they'd be there for me. But, despite all that, loneliness persisted. Reading, going for walks, watching TV, nothing seemed to satisfy my lonely spirit; I didn't know what to do to find peace.

With each passing year, feelings of being alone intensified and negatively affected my outlook on everything I did. Every day, my spirit quickly became drained of enthusiasm; the daily schedule became a tedious grind. I had only emptiness inside.

But my constant run-ins with the pillars of the communities, my refusal to be a more active member of the Knights, complaints to the bishop about something I had said in my homily, or about those I was visiting and those that I wasn't, hadn't held me in good standing with my superiors. I was becoming as demanding as others had been on me, paternalistic and patriarchal, full of negative energy, defensive, self-righteous and arrogant.

As always, I knew there was something different about me. I had kept my secret throughout my seminary studies and into my priesthood, never realizing that it was the most important gift of my life, the pearl that I needed to discover and disclose, and in doing so to find the connection and sexual intimacy I longed for — but could never have within the Catholic institution.

I had to face the fact that I'd had trouble with parish ministry from the beginning. My spirit and my body regularly tried to tell me I wouldn't find acceptance, a sense of belonging, fulfillment, nor even an honest relationship with God as a gay male in a Catholic institution, let alone as a gay parish priest. I developed health problems regularly, usually at the same time I was having a conflict with the church hierarchy.

I asked for a year off in 1990, ten years after the crisis in Brandon, when I'd had my first break from parish ministry, taking refuge in a basement room in a big house in the Wolseley area of Winnipeg.

Coming to Terms

In November 1990, at a Catholic Clergy Study Days event, a psychologist presented the four levels of burnout, Level 4 requiring chemical intervention. I was at the end of Level 3 and heading for Level 4. I discussed it with the bishop, who said he'd get back to me. When we met again, he asked, "Ray, how would you feel about seeing a psychiatrist?"

I think it was spiritual intervention that immediately inspired me to ask, "Bishop, will you be willing to go along with whatever the psychiatrist suggests?"

He agreed that he would, and in early 1991 the psychiatrist recommended I take the year off as I had wanted. The bishop, in turn, asked that I agree to see the psychiatrist on a regular basis.

But I was not yet quite through with parish ministry. I wasn't long back in Winnipeg after leaving Dunrea, when I was asked to take on an interim placement at an ethnic parish in the city. As I walked into my first Sunday service in that church, a large statue of Mary stood at the entrance, flanked by candles on both sides and in front. The plaster mould of her toes had been worn almost completely away from having been touched and fondled so much. Almost every candle was lit, the small ones, at twenty-five cents each, and the larger ones at a dollar each.

As I began the service, some parishioners stayed at the statue praying rather than participate with the congregation. As soon as the mass ended and the final hymn was beginning, many headed for the exits, others went to pray at the various statues, others started mingling and talking. I found the entire experience unsettling. Though they were kind, generous and thoughtful people, and I did feel their sincere intentions, I was not used to such religiosity. There was nothing spiritual about the rituals, nor the Sunday services; they were mere duties to be performed. With that experience, my nagging discomfort and confusion around parish ministry was revived.

At our first meeting, the psychiatrist asked me to go to the Refit Centre in Winnipeg where I was wired up and put through a series of stress tests. The following day, I was told to rest for the next few weeks because my blood pressure was so dangerously high I was in danger of having a fatal heart attack — the result of forcing myself to stay extremely busy and not taking care of myself. Following his orders, my body and mind were forced to stop running in all directions. My body was giving me an ultimatum! *"Stop, or I will shut-down!"* Though I felt fine, the warning had to be taken seriously.

Two weeks later, after starting an exercise program at the Refit Centre, I returned to see the psychiatrist. He began by saying, "Ray, you have to learn how to be good to yourself."

"I don't know what you mean," I replied, holding back tears.

"I know you don't," he said.

I knew what the words meant, but didn't know how they applied to me, yet I knew they probably did. I had an excuse for everything he suggested. Go for walks? "To where?"

Find a hobby? "Don't have time."

Develop relationships? "I deal with people all day."

Read? "I read a lot of articles and pastoral books."

Then he asked me to treat myself to a movie, a meal, a concert.

At forty-one, I had come to a critical point in my life and would have to face many issues. The tears wouldn't be held back. To better get in touch with my feelings, I was asked to join support groups in which my feelings could be shared and explored, and to continue seeing the psychiatrist every two weeks.

I wasn't an addict but I attended weekly meetings of alcoholics anonymous, sexaholics anonymous, and co-dependency anonymous. I also joined the Manitoba Men's Network. Men were divided into random groups of about eight and met regularly to share whatever they wanted to share about their lives and their feelings. I remained with the same group for several years. I also joined the Winnipeg Art Gallery and went to weekly Tai Chi lessons.

The support groups used the language of helplessness, power-lessness, impulsiveness, manipulation, perfectionism and control, all of which I could relate to. I hadn't come out as a gay man even to myself, let alone to any group but, through all of it, I finally began to understand and confront my own sexual orientation. Still, I kept it secret.

I also joined an alternative healing group, which was a very eclectic group; we met monthly, stressing holistic health, using various professional groups, cultures, ideologies, religions and sects. A one day workshop on holistic health helped me put a structure to, and gain further clarification around my shrink's comment that I needed to learn how to be good to myself.

The spiritual language of being present to myself and others that I learned struck me profoundly. It became an important element in the clinical training that I'd begin in 1995.

Over the course of a few weeks, my interest was aroused and I went to a bookstore and chose a book that caught my attention on the topic of narcissism, *The Drama of the Gifted Child*, by Alice Miller. Then I wanted to go somewhere to reflect and asked to spend November and December at the Trappist Monastery north of Toronto. Once again, I found myself living with monks as I had in the summer of 1967. This time they were busy making Christmas fruit cakes and, just like at the previous monastery, I worked in the bakery.

Those two months proved very difficult for me. That monastery, which has since closed, was in the middle of 350 acres of beautiful rolling hills with great walking paths, tall pine trees and lots of deer. When it snowed, the landscape became overwhelmingly beautiful. In that winter paradise, nature allowed me my first opportunity to scream at the top of my lungs over what I felt were my many losses.

Miller's book, *The Drama of the Gifted Child*, was shocking and surprising... as if the author knew me personally and perhaps had lived as an invisible person at my side during every moment of my childhood. I didn't know what to make of that. Every sentence, evaluation and observation made it seem as if she also knew my mother intimately. But before the book, I had never thought of my mother in that particular way, nor had I ever heard someone speak about me in the same way, but as I read, I knew it all to be true.

Reading *The Drama of the Gifted Child* was like watching a movie about my own childhood. At the end of each section, I had to go into the woods to cry and scream. Sometimes I felt I would lose my breath completely and drop where I stood. I felt vulnerable, exposed, and yet not alone. I felt the presence of God in the woods, accepting me, allowing me to cry and scream, day after day, week after week.

Sometimes I returned exhausted, yet grateful for the silence of my room and an opportunity to sleep early. God had given me the time to read, cry and pray, with no one expecting anything from me. Several times a day, I would do just that, cry my thanks to God for that sacred time and place.

Alice Miller writes, "If both spiritual hunger and dependency on human loving are denied or rejected, the only thing left is narcissism." At first those words haunted me, and then they became part of my spiritual journey.

Miller's book brought me to the realization that I had been an emotionally abused child. I came to accept that my parents never intended to emotionally abuse me, but they had. They did the best they could with what they had and knew, and had the best intentions at heart. I perceived my childhood much differently after reading *The Drama of the Gifted Child*.

As I came to understand my spiritual journey, I accepted the grace that my parents had been for me because without them, and my experiences, this book wouldn't have been possible.

From the very beginning, I had no choice but to comply totally with the needs and feelings of my mother and ignore my own. I'd never questioned my version of the happy childhood I supposedly had enjoyed but, with hindsight, the more I learned to follow my impulses, to express my own thoughts, to believe in what I believed in, and not in what I had been taught and told to believe in, the weaker became my allegiance to the Catholic institution, and the more compassionate and understanding I became towards my mother. Unfortunately, the opportunity for my mother and me to speak about it was never possible.

My mother had said to me, as we stood before her own mother lying in a casket, "I don't know why I can't cry."

But I knew why she couldn't cry. She had been raised as I had been raised. She was looking at the woman in that casket who had taken her childhood from her, who had used her daughter to get respect, just as I was standing beside the woman who had similarly used me.

Growing up, I'd never experienced natural contact with my own emotions and wishes, which would have given me strength and self-esteem. I needed to experience feelings, to be sad, despairing, or in need of help, without the fear of making my mother insecure.

But that had never been possible.

I needed to have allowed myself to be afraid when I felt threatened or angry when my wishes weren't fulfilled. I needed to know not only what I didn't want, but also what I did, and to express those desires irrespective of whether I would be loved or hated by my mother for doing so. But that had never been possible.

Finally realizing these things — my losses — I went for walks far into the woods where, with no one around, I screamed and screamed till near exhaustion. The woods enabled me to expose myself to emotions that had welled up out of my earliest childhood and to experience the helplessness and ambivalence of that period. Clinging tendencies and feelings of helplessness mingled with long damned-up rage against my mother, who hadn't been available to me.

The monastic environment allowed me to finally experience the pain, and to give up the old illusion of a happy childhood. And through it all, I grew up. I discovered a new need, a need to live according to my true self and no longer allow myself to be forced to earn love.

The monks always got together on Christmas Eve, after evening prayers, for a special celebration. In the privacy of their monastery a tree was decorated, tables covered with wines, cheeses and goodies. Everyone spoke freely with one another. In that rarefied atmosphere of seasonal joy, I took the opportunity to thank them for their hospitality.

Because they weren't used to such socializing, the evening ended gradually, and late. The following morning, a beautiful Christmas mass was held. The Christmas tree remained lit and the rest of the day was kept in silence and simplicity, in sharp contrast to the following day, Boxing Day, in downtown Toronto.

Before leaving the monastery, I cherished one last walk in the woods. I felt a deep peace knowing my mother would no longer have emotional and psychological control over me. And I felt a deep sadness knowing that at the same time, she'd never understand my independence and never accept my behaviours, my thinking, my feelings, my emotions and my desires.

I felt a deep gratitude to God for having given me the opportunity that allowed me to experience a rebirth in my own life, a gift that I will always cherish.

Upon my return to Winnipeg in January 1992, I embarked on what I hoped would be a better experience of parish ministry.

The Oblate Fathers had ministered among the aboriginal and Inuit people in our diocese for many years, but with recruitment declining, the need for our diocesan priests to serve these communities increased. With few diocesan priests culturally prepared to serve aboriginal communities, my request to the bishop to take studies in native spirituality at the University of British Columbia and to minister among the aboriginal people in our diocese was welcomed. Remembering how much I had enjoyed the simplicity of the religious and spiritual lives of the Inuit, I was very pleased as well.

June and July of 1992 were spent studying with aboriginal people from all over the world and learning a great deal from them as they shared their rituals, spiritual beliefs, customs and tribal links. There was a spirit of tolerance and respect among us for their belief in the power of dreams, visions, rituals, fasting and the little people.

Upon my return, I was asked to be the administrator of five communities located two hours north of Winnipeg, one of which was aboriginal — the Lake Manitoba Reserve. I felt very comfortable with the aboriginal people, but as I was leaving the reserve one evening during a heavy rain, which made the road very muddy and slippery, I suddenly felt a strong need to pull over to the side of the road. The car came to a stop and I began to cry uncontrollably.

"Thank you, God for bringing me home," I kept saying. But that northern reserve was not my home.

After some time, I managed to pull myself together and go home, but I was on the road again the next evening on my way to a powwow.

When I arrived, I found only an elder sitting by a large fire that was encircled by benches waiting for the absent crowds.

"Where is everyone?" I asked.

"It was cancelled because we thought it would start to rain again," the elder said, then asked me, "Did you see what was in the sky when you arrived?"

"No."

"A double rainbow... I think the reason I was called to stay seated here was to meet you," he said.

We sat quietly for a few minutes, and then I asked him if I could tell him about what had happened to me the previous evening. He was okay with that, so I did. Afterwards, he said, "You have probably been among our people in a previous life and your spirit is now back among its people."

Somehow, that made sense to me; I had always felt comfortable among aboriginal people.

"You are being called to be a warrior of the rainbow," the elder added.

At the time, I didn't understand what that meant and we didn't talk a lot more, preferring to sit quietly and enjoy the fire before we left.

Most people in that aboriginal community were not preoccupied with church regulations. The dominant preoccupation was with problems of addictions and domestic abuse, which were rampant. Families were divided for many reasons: because of separate ties to other denominations, political and legal struggles within the community and young people being attracted to lifestyles depicted in television advertising. Many had also struggled with the effects that the Canadian residential school system had on them.

Some were grateful for the education and support they had received in that system because they needed it to enter southern society. But for others, the residential system had been abusive, inflicting humiliation and pain on them, in part, through being told their aboriginal beliefs and practices were not of God and that they'd have to forsake their aboriginal language, culture, customs, traditions and spirituality if they wanted to be pleasing to God. As a gay priest with the burden of his own secret, I could relate to their struggle.

Many aboriginal parents had been left with feelings of shame, resentment, guilt and the hope that their children would be able to "get done" in a church, as they had been as children. Many were burdened by the resurgence of their own spirituality and rituals, which were no longer considered illegal and which were calling them to their root experiences of a relationship with God. Families were torn once again between wanting to experience what they had been taught was pagan, and the fear of rejection by some self-righteous family members who had come to believe the old ways were, indeed, truly not of God.

My parents had offered their children a Catholic faith foundation that they had hoped we would also cherish. I could understand those parents who found it very painful to see their children making different choices in the practice of their faith. Parents and guardians would ask themselves where they had gone wrong, and if God would judge them for the choices their children were making. Would God forgive their children and continue to bless them? Would He one day allow their children to be with Him in Heaven?

We had imposed our faith on them as a gift and now we were making them feel guilty for not continuing to go along with what we'd been asking of them.

They had seen us as punishing their children by not letting them receive the rites of passage. I was once again getting very tired of this kind of church heavy handedness, not to mention all the same old issues with parish ministry, which persisted. I was determined to keep my sanity this time and, although I very much related to the aboriginal people, I decided to move on. However, I was determined to right what I saw as a major wrong before I left.

When it came time for me to leave the area, I let it be known that the Sunday before my departure I would baptize the children who had not yet been baptized, knowing that this would probably be their only chance to "get done." I asked that a family member attend three meetings to instruct and prepare them, and that the family member agree to share the information with anyone wanting to be baptized. Godparents and sponsors had to be chosen, copies of birth certificates were needed, a white stole had to be made for each person being baptized, and the families needed to organize a reception in the hall after the service.

For my part, I needed to organize the service, prepare someone to write up the certificates, and ask singers and musicians from the aboriginal parish in Winnipeg to help us . The instructions were well-received and the people were excited as everyone prepared for the big day. But I had seen people's plans change quickly on the reserve so one question played on my mind throughout all the preparations — how many would actually show up?

Thankfully, the weather turned out to be beautiful because it was, indeed, a busy day. The church and reception hall were ready and the ladies had completed preparations. The singers were in place and practicing before the service. I had everything set up and ready to go.

Then it started... car after car arrived. Within minutes children were everywhere and everyone was dressed in their best attire. The babies, some of the children, and a few adults who were to be baptized, stood out from the crowd with their white stoles around their necks; dozens and dozens of white stoles dotted the congregation. Literally hundreds of people gathered... and I felt a bit like John the Baptiser.

The service was organized chaos. Everyone seemed so happy and excited. I could tell they knew exactly what was happening as they responded to questions and instructions. With so many people, it took a few hours before we got to the reception, which consisted of an abundance of aboriginal cuisine. The singers came to the hall to offer entertainment, as did almost every child on the reserve. The adults, especially the elders, were very grateful. It was a service I'll never forget.

Many aboriginal people knew how the Catholic Church felt about many of their beliefs and practices, but rather than argue with the hierarchy, they kept their culture and beliefs close to their hearts, which was their way of being in a spiritual relationship with God, whom they called Manitou.

I have always felt for people trying to fit in because I've never been able to. I've always identified with people who have a unique relationship with God because I believe that's what I've always had. And I have always felt for people who have been made to feel guilty for how they live because I, with my fantasies and knowing the church would disapprove, have always felt guilty about my secret.

Aboriginal issues played a significant part in my spiritual journey, and through the experiences I had among them I redefined my relationship with God — now a relationship outside the institution of the church.

As a priest, I was regularly presented with a steady stream of documents from the Vatican covering almost every imaginable aspect of life. In late 1989, for example, the Pope's head of the Congregation for the Doctrine of the Faith, his "guardian of orthodoxy" (Joseph Ratzinger), issued a document warning Roman Catholics that Zen, yoga, and transcendental meditation could "degenerate into a cult of the body." It was followed by a day-long workshop for all the priests in the diocese.

The priest conducting the workshop had been presented as an expert on the topic of cults and the New Age Movement. I remember being more afraid of him than anything he had to say. His job was to convince us priests of the dangers, so we, in turn, could enlighten our parishioners.

Then, in late 1992, the institution released its "New Catechism," the first since the Council of Trent in 1566. It was hailed by Pope John Paul II as a major event in the Roman Catholic Church.

It included birth control as a matter of self-discipline; infertile periods as acceptable; ordination limited to baptized men, in keeping with Christ's own example; and the ordination of women as impossible. Homosexuality went against natural law, while homosexuals were to be treated with compassion and fairness and urged to be chaste.

Without knowing the story, on May 5, 1995, I saw the movie *The Priest*. It depicts a gay priest caught by the police in a sexual encounter. His bishop and parishioners react badly. I sat stunned and numb, watching what seemed to be my own life on film — other viewers left the theatre in anger and disgust.

"I must not be alone," I thought, wondering if the movie had been based on a real person. Leaving the theatre, I once again felt the loneliness of having no one to share the experience with and was filled with the fear of realizing that if my bishop ever found out about me, I'd probably be treated the same way as the poor fellow in the movie.

That film had an overwhelming impact on me. I felt great fear, but also encouragement because I felt more confident that I wasn't the only one with the secret.

In July of 1995, a priest named Father Henry suggested I have a talk with the Catholic chaplain at the prison in Headingley, just outside Winnipeg.

"Why do you want me to see him?" I asked. "I don't know him."

"Just ask to see him," he said.

A few days later, I met the chaplain and he asked why I had come.

"Father Henry asked me to see you, but I don't know why."

"Ray, tell me your story," he said.

He patiently listened to me, then said, "Sounds similar to my own story. Have you ever considered being a chaplain?"

"As a parish priest, I've never seen it as an option," I replied.

He then sent out a fax and shortly afterwards received a response, which he handed asked me to give to the bishop. It asked that I be allowed to take clinical training to become a chaplain.

"The bishop won't agree," I told him. "The last thing he said to me was, 'The next time you come here, it'll be on my terms, not yours'."

The chaplain asked me to swallow my pride and make an appointment to see the bishop anyway. I did as he suggested.

As I walked into the chancery, the only thing missing was a red carpet. I was greeted like the prodigal son returning from a life of debauchery and squandering — the squandering part didn't apply to me.

Everyone greeted and welcomed me back. After a fraternal hug from the bishop and an offer of a cup of coffee, I was welcomed into his office. He seemed genuinely pleased to see me again.

After about a fifteen-minute update, I showed him the note that the prison chaplain had given me. His narrowed his eyes and his face got red. He put the paper on his desk and stood with his right hand outstretched towards me and his index finger pointing directly between my eyes.

"You get the f— out of here," he screamed at the top of his lungs.

I stood frozen for a moment, and then he continued.

"Come back in three days and I'll tell you where you're going."

Humiliated and stunned, I left his office under the glare of the others present, who looked at me in silence and dismay.

I went to sleep early that night, still stunned, tired and confused. The following morning at about 8 a.m., the phone rang; it was the bishop, and my heart leapt to my throat.

Sounding very distraught, he said, "Ray, could you please come to the office as soon as possible... today?"

Half an hour later, I arrived and was offered another cup of coffee and wondered if I would have time to finish it before he threw me out again. He was visibly shaken and had difficulty speaking.

"I had a dream last night," he began. Pacing back and forth in front of his desk, he continued. "In my dream, I spent the entire night in hell."

This was not the time to offer my opinion, though I was sorely tempted.

"I'd been sent there because I had refused to help a brother priest," he said.

That dream must have been as clear to him as Joseph's had been in the scriptures when he was asked to flee to Egypt.

As he slowly sat down, he apologized, signed the chaplain's note and added, "I'll be phoning the coordinator of chaplains to ask him to help you in any way he can, and the diocese will pay for your studies."

I made it. My coffee was down to the last drop and I was still there.

With a thank-you and a handshake, I was once again on my way out, and once again, to the surprise of the mesmerized staff, I was leaving as stunned as I had been the day before. Inside I felt much better and phoned the chaplain to give him the news as soon as I got home.

When I later recounted the incident to my new bishop in 2002, his response was, "Well, it makes for a good story."

"*Whatever!*" I thought and prepared to begin my new studies.

Chaplaincy

During my clinical pastoral education studies, I didn't have to deal with the parish politics that emanated from the tensions between the demands of the hierarchy and the ritual needs of parishioners. Most importantly, I was free of the helpless frustration of being in the middle, trying to be at the service of both groups.

I was about to study the writings of Henri J. M. Nouwen, who had died in 1996 while vacationing in Holland where he was born in 1932. A priest and professor at Yale and Harvard, Nouwen was also the man I had met at the Trappist monastery in 1967 and was later described to me as one of the best known and most honoured spiritual writers of our time.

Through dozens of books, such as *Reaching Out* and *The Wounded Healer*, Nouwen invited countless people to enter the spiritual life more deeply. Some of his important endeavours had been in early support of the civil rights movement, his engagement in the cause of peace, and work with disabled members of the L'Arche community.

He had always been immersed in the social, as well as the spiritual, dimensions of the gospel.

In 1985, Nouwen wrote that women had a real call to ministry and that homosexuals had a unique vocation in the Christian community. After he died, we began hearing about his sexual orientation. I'm sure he was only too aware of the scandal that his private life would have created and how he would have been treated had that fact been revealed while he was alive.

The first basic unit of my clinical studies took place at Headingley Correctional Centre just west of Winnipeg. The second, and my first advanced units were held at the Health Sciences Centre in Winnipeg. Issues addressed included one's role as a chaplain, one's identity and the meaning of professional presence and due process. I had to learn what it meant to be present to someone and not to escape as soon as I felt rejected or intimidated, or as soon as I was finished with my business. I had to learn to sit with someone without expectations or agenda.

When those studies were completed, my supervisor from the hospital gave me the following evaluation:

Theologically, Ray is well-grounded and solidly identified. He is a compassionate and pastoral Roman Catholic Priest who loves and respects his church, but suffers from what he experiences to be its rigid institutional structures. He claims his autonomy and authority by offering a non-judgmental and compassionate ministry to those individuals and groups who are in need of this comfort. His theological perspectives were the broadest within the peer group and he has modelled this kind of openness for his peers as well as for our department. At the same time, he values and generously offers the healing sacraments of his religious tradition when they are requested. I affirm Ray's theological and pastoral stance as I believe they converge well with the demands of the ministry of chaplaincy.

Chaplaincy clients often want spiritual comfort, not just religious rituals. That was refreshing and exciting for me, yet unsettling. A transition was taking place within me that I didn't fully understand. I had thought that words such as faith, religion and spirituality were terms for one and the same reality.

As a Catholic, I had been influenced and directed into various forms of spirituality through the works of a number of Catholic writers: St. Francis, St. Theresa, St. Augustine, St. John of the Cross, St. Bernard, St. Benedict, and St. Ignatius, to name a few. These men and women had written at times in history when the Catholic Church had ultimate control and power, and within a culture that saw virtue and sainthood in practicing complete obedience. For me, the language was of submission, guilt, obedience and self-denial.

Since childhood, my spiritual hunger for answers to the many questions I had about beliefs and doctrines made me feel I was just difficult, contrary, and somehow unfaithful. I had no difficulty believing in God, but I had trouble with the notion that I had to believe all the doctrines for the sake of my soul.

In both the hospital and corrections, however, I spoke with clients who had very different spiritual views from those I had been raised with, and from those of former Catholic parishioners. Within chaplaincy training group dynamics, I was able to share my own views without judgment, suspicion, ridicule or scandal, and began to realize that my spirituality looked beyond organized religion. In my thirst to satisfy my spiritual hunger while still accepting my Roman Catholic faith, it was refreshing to question and articulate my own views, and receive the feedback and support from others.

Nothing remained a greater human mystery, nor a more popular topic of daily discussion at the Health Sciences Centre than death. We all know we're going to die and there's nothing we can do to prevent it. The only questions are when, and whether death marks the termination of our existence. There is much bewilderment about the reality of death and what, if anything, lies beyond it.

My hospital experience showed me that life can exceed our desire for it. Consequently, an increasingly important question for many is the question of how people can die with dignity, including the right to die when they choose.

Perhaps surprisingly to some, something else that helped us understand the meaning of life was the New Age Movement. It was often spoken about, along with other fringe activities, such as meditation, astrology, tarot cards, reincarnation, out of-body experiences and dream analysis.

The New Age Movement had become a significant spiritual movement. It focused on the tapping of one's potential, personal spirituality, the spirit world, the oneness of creation, the limitless potential of humanity, the possibility of transforming the self, and today's world, into something better.

As one of my term positions while studying at the hospital, I was assigned to the intensive care unit and asked to develop an in-service for the staff on spirituality and wellness. The outline I developed stated that God calls us to be healthy, and that we're healthy when we're in harmony within ourselves — within the relationship between body, mind and spirit. We are in health when there's harmony in our relationship with others and with our higher power. The prophet Jesus said the same thing 2,000 years ago when he referred to "loving God with all our being, and our neighbour as ourselves."

After completing the course in clinical pastoral education, I was hired by Corrections Manitoba as a staff chaplain at Headingley. For the first time in my priesthood, I was free from parish routine and could be more open about God and who I really am. In my previous religious life, I had felt stifled by the church. Ironically, I had to land in a prison to feel free.

My work involved counselling inmates who were dealing with a number of different issues and crises. Though the work was difficult, I found it rewarding, personally challenging and spiritually fulfilling.

Chaplaincy serves the spiritual needs of individuals in a wide variety of institutions: hospitals, universities, the military and prisons. Although endorsed by a particular faith community, chaplains serve the institution that employs them, not just their respective churches. As a chaplain, I had a foot in two worlds; I was a government employee with my own salary, living independently from the diocese, but still a priest. I was living a celibate life in a secular world — but was I?

I had been a closeted gay priest for twenty-five years, careful to keep my secret, to separate my various lives. But living one step removed from the church in my own apartment, away from the fishbowl of parish life, I began to live more openly. I felt a tremendous sense of independence from the bishop, from church activities, and from parishioners' expectations. After all, prison inmates accepted me as I was.

I felt free to go to gay bars, meet other men for sexual encounters and make a life for myself as part of the gay community. I joined LAMBDA, attended a gay spiritual support group and went to Gay Pride events. But I was naïve to think I could live such a lifestyle and be a priest at the same time without the two worlds eventually colliding.

I felt I had been called to the priesthood, and had found a way of living out my priesthood as a chaplain, but my new-found "out" life was just as important to me as my priesthood. I began to think of my new life as an expansion of my secret with God. However, secrets have a way of not staying secret.

The Hierarchy
(the one percent who can wear a pointed hat in church – called a Mitre)

In 1995, I was introduced to Diarmuid O'Murchu's book *Reclaiming Spirituality*, which gave me a language to help me articulate my spiritual experience. He spoke of the power and control of the Catholic Institution as being in the hands of the hierarchy, which makes up as he wrote, less than one percent of the church, with the remainder being the faithful. It helped me understand that a new era was upon us, an era in which many would no longer accept being controlled by guilt and shame and intimidation.

I adopted this reference but I speak of the one percent as being all those who wear pointed hats in church. They are the only ones with power and control. It's my view that the remainders of the hierarchy, the ordained priests, are a subculture separate from the one percent, and also separate from the faithful and the religious brothers and nuns who make up the remaining ninety-nine percent.

In 2002, I attended a workshop for service providers in Winnipeg on domestic abuse. It dealt with the theoretical background to abuse. At that workshop, I became aware of a language that enabled me to understand my entire spiritual journey; a language that defined the following terms:

- abuse – doing something that inspires fear
- control – a choice that is aggressive or subtle
- power – the ability to enforce control
- empowerment – the ability to do something for oneself

An abusive relationship consists of one person relentlessly pursuing a position of power and control relative to another person until an imbalance of power results. Control is accomplished through intimidation and the exploitation of vulnerability, creating for the victim a chronic state of fear and anxiety. The means used may be aggressive or seemingly passive in nature. Considering this, I see my relationship with my bishop as having been emotionally abusive, not healthy.

The one percent, in holding authority, status and wealth, are ensured power over their priests and the ninety-nine percent. They hold authority because of our willingness to submit to them.

I would never have even considered questioning the authority of the one percent because I was totally convinced that what the one percent said was part of their duty to ensure the "True Faith" and protect the "Chair of Peter" (the papacy). The idea of questioning any of that would have been seen as heresy.

The one percent continues to ignore the fact that the majority of Catholics are not much for the credibility of the Catholic Institution's teachings if the vast majority of its members think, judge, and act as though the norms don't really exist. In looking at the subjective state of mind of the Catholics in my parishes who practised contraception, quite clearly in good conscience, it follows that if their consciences were clear, they were not committing a sin. They most certainly were not confessing what they were doing as a sin. For this kind of thinking not to succeed, the one percent, through the obedience of its priests, has to keep the ninety-nine percent in guilt and shame to maintain its position.

I now understood why the one percent is so fearful. Collectively, it can only listen and accept someone who is totally submissive and obedient, and who can be kept in line.

The one percent wants to be respected and obeyed. They feel they're in power by the will of God and, therefore, are in the right. They feel that society and our culture is immoral, and that it's their responsibility and divine right to remind us what God wants us to do, which is also the self-righteous and defensive stance of all who abuse.

Rather than argue with this arrogance, many are leaving in silence and anger at being kept in guilt and fear to be intimidated into blind obedience. In our early history, popes and governments worked together, and then came the separation of church and state.

In our century, the one percent influenced the number of children a family should have, who to vote for, and stated that sex was only for procreation in a family context between a man and a woman. Concerning remarriage, the one percent has had to allow annulments, or even fewer financial supporters would sit in churches.

Signs were there in 2002 that indicated that something was about to happen. I was hearing how a number of priests and nuns were not allowed to speak out publicly. The most painful example was that of Sister Jeannine Gramick and Father Robert Nugent, who had worked for decades in ministry with gay and lesbian Catholics. The Vatican, in silencing them and no longer allowing them to minister to homosexual people, was discriminating in the worst way.

The one percent keeps using scandal as a reason for its persecution of theologians and others. Yet studies show that more people were scandalized by the actions of the one percent than by those who supposedly caused scandal. Despite the fact that Nugent spoke on "silent witness" and Gramick drew on official church documents for the right of church members to speak their opinions and to form their consciences, their arguments were refuted by the one percent and they were silenced.

This came as a great disappointment but no surprise to me. It is the inevitable consequence for anyone (abused spouse or priest) who tries to confront the abuser, especially if the abuser is homophobic as well.

Many priests can relate to the pain of having no one to speak to about their feelings of isolation, humiliation, helplessness, fear and vulnerability. Many of us have seen the impact on others. Many of us have been silenced and have seen how the situation has affected our thinking. Yet the Vatican doesn't hesitate to sanction apparent dissenters to its position on celibacy, premarital sex, homosexuality, contraception, euthanasia, creation-centred spirituality, and other issues. Dissent from its official teaching on moral issues is severely censured.

The one percent remains in denial by labeling all gay priests as potential pedophiles in order to entirely avoid the topics of homosexuality and women in ministry. But these issues won't go away, even if some among the clergy and the ninety-nine percent do move on.

So why is there abuse? The issue touches many of us on a very personal level. It has become an overwhelming social problem because it's surrounded by shame and secrecy. The abusers have protected themselves by using denial, which protects them from ever thinking that what they do should cause them to feel any shame. When they are challenged to confront their issues, they take a defensive position, reject the idea, and aren't open to change because they're in denial about their abusive behaviour. Unfortunately, their denial interferes with them ever understanding the issue.

My present experience is very new to me. I've never experienced freedom before. Using the analogy of the fishbowl, when dumped into a tub of water I swam beyond my familiar and secure social context. I was literally in uncharted waters. I wasn't afraid because I've always enjoyed moving beyond boundaries, evidenced by my readily taking on new parishes and projects. But in all my parishes and projects, the one percent made their presence felt through their expectations and additional boundaries. Their religiosity stifled me and prevented me from feeling happy and free.

It's my observation and experience that the one percent, through no ill-will on their part, is incapable of accepting the gifts of the language of the heart, passion and imagination that women and gay priests could offer the institution. Why? Because the one percent is collectively in the mindset of an abuser and, hence, remains in denial.

Coming Out

Acknowledging that I was gay to some friends included socializing in the gay community, joining gay social activities, gay spirituality discussion groups and attending gay lectures and discussions on coming out and the gay lifestyle. Being a chaplain and a Roman Catholic priest, I was putting myself at risk of exposure, intimidation and public scandal.

Shortly after moving into my apartment, I received a call from a former acquaintance.

Tom, who had moved to West some years previous, was the son of a woman who'd been very helpful to me in one of my previous parishes.

"My friend and I are going to visit my mother and wondered if we could visit you in Winnipeg on the way?" he asked.

"Sure Tom," I answered with excitement. "Will you be in Winnipeg for a few days?" I asked, with hope in my voice.

"Would you have room for us?"

"Sure, I have a fold-out futon in the living room," I said.

"Great! We'll call you in a few days, Father Ray."

Our first evening together happened to be a Friday and they told me about their plans.

"We want to go to a gay bar and we'd like you to come with us," Tom said.

I hadn't come out to him, but he later confessed that his "gaydar" had figured me out not long after I had first met him and had spent time being supportive of him, which he had appreciated. They were content to wait for me to finally come out to them, which I did. The revelation had them gleaming with the self-satisfaction of knowing their gaydar had been accurate.

That Friday evening however, I said, "No, I'm sure you two will have a great time... I'll give you my spare key."

But they wouldn't take no for an answer. After wasting some time trying to reason with them, I succumbed and went along.

As we entered the bar, I was almost immediately approached by a husky, muscular stud, who later became one of my regular visitors.

"Ray" (which I insisted on being called while we were together), "you don't waste much time, do you?" Tom observed.

After the weekend with them, I decided to call Suzette and come out to her as well. She was the daughter of one of the families I had befriended and was living in Winnipeg and had come out to me. I desperately needed someone to share with and I knew I could trust her. Afterwards, we hugged and cried and became close friends, indulging in regular coffee and chocolate cookie encounters.

She's always been a very attractive woman, able to turn the head of every man who crosses her path. When we were together and she'd notice that, she'd smile at me and say, "Ray, he's all yours."

Our conversations would have shocked our parents, embarrassed some of our friends and aroused other gays.

Through gay chat lines, my encounters were mostly one-night stands, though some became friends and others became regulars. Going to socials, the bars and bath houses became lucrative in terms of gay contact, but none of the encounters developed into relationships because, as a priest, I couldn't chance being in a long-term relationship. However, I never admitted that to any of the men who expressed a long-term interest. Of those I did tell about my being a priest, some were shocked into flight while others felt even more comfortable with me.

In time, that unavailability — my inability to make a commitment with anyone — caused intense loneliness, even in the midst of all my one-night stands and regulars. I always knew that at the end of the day, even if someone stayed over for the night, he wouldn't be there to comfort and support me and would never be my significant other, which was what my soul had always pained for. Henri Nouwen would have known and understood the pain of my experience.

In May, 1997, I was hired full-time in prison chaplaincy. My priesthood protected my sexual orientation in that anyone with suspicions about me wouldn't say anything to me about them. Many, especially Catholics, thought priests had a special supernatural grace to suppress their human feelings and needs while others thought of priests as eunuchs, or at least asexual. But those who knew differently spoke behind my back and among themselves. Being exposed as a gay male in a male prison by some guard or an inmate's gaydar could have been difficult and dangerous because of homophobia.

Because sexual contacts in prison were always discreet and often engaged in to have human needs met, they were not necessarily an indication of sexual orientation. When someone spoke about their sexual orientation, my calm acceptance was supportive and affirming for them. On a number of occasions, an inmate would say, "You seem to understand me," and I'd think, *"If you only knew."*

It was during this time that I met a one-night stand. He asked that we remain friends. We began meeting every few weeks and he became a valuable and knowledgeable mentor within the gay community. As a gay activist, he was very aware of the gay scene in the community.

After a few months, when he said he appreciated our friendship, I began to feel very guilty because I had not told him I was a priest out of fear of possible rejection and of scandalizing him, which actually would have been laughable.

"I have something I want to say to you that is very difficult for me," I nervously managed one day.

"We'll talk about it the next time we meet," he replied bluntly.

Two weeks later, as he made himself comfortable on the couch with a Corona in hand, he asked, "Well, what did you want to tell me that was going to be so difficult to say?"

I thought I was going to pass out but there was no backing away. "I'm a priest!" I blurted out.

"That's it? That's the secret you found so hard to tell me? Aren't all priests gay?"

After a few hours of painful disclosure, he asked. "Promise me that you won't do your priest thing at my funeral, should I die before you."

"I promise."

When there's a hole in a dike and then it finally breaks, it's difficult to hold the water back. A fellow priest, to whom I had come out, told me about a convocation of gay priests that he wanted to attend in the United States. I asked for more details and, without telling anyone, made plans to attend.

Because of the flood of the century in 1997 in Winnipeg, our formal church retreat was cancelled and we were asked to make our own arrangements. I asked the bishop for permission to attend a retreat in the States and, since I was not asking for financial assistance and was going during my holiday time, he gave his permission and no further questions were asked.

When we arrived, as I walked into a room of a few hundred gay priests, tears came to my eyes.

"Are you alright?" someone asked.

"Have you any idea how I feel right now?" I sobbed.

"Until recently, I had thought I was the only gay priest in the world."

"We've all felt that way at one time," he replied.

The weekend was electrifying; the liturgies, the speakers, the sharing, the sexual energy — it was all so overwhelming. The retreat helped me to know, accept and celebrate who I am. I'd always known that I was different.

In 1999, I attended gay pride celebrations in Toronto, Vancouver and Montreal, but in Winnipeg, I often felt judged and unaccepted, which made my coming out process even more difficult. To many in the gay community who felt like outsiders in the church, I personified the institution. Some saw me as living in two different worlds. And I feared scandalizing those who recognized me as much as I feared being rejected or outed to the hierarchy.

At bars and other social events, I just wanted to be among like-minded people but often felt like an outsider to the faith community, like a leper.

My father died that same year. My siblings didn't know what to say nor what to expect from each other. We had become strangers to one another.

Dad had had a strong devotion to the Mother of Jesus so I asked the church soloist to sing "Ave Maria." It was very moving. And out of respect for me as a priest, the bishop sat near the altar throughout the service. Dad's spirit felt privileged and grateful to his son.

Mother stayed strong, as usual, keeping her feelings and thoughts to herself. My heart went out to her and I did my best to help her be comfortable and cared for. I ignored her comments and did what I felt needed to be done. Leaving was painful for me, knowing we had grown apart and feeling that I couldn't do anything about it.

On my return to Winnipeg, I offered to assist part-time at St. Ann's, an inner city parish that had just lost its priest. I enjoyed the people and looked forward to Sunday worship, which was the only time I could offer the community because of my full-time work at the prison. But, once again unable to live up to the expectations of the pillars of the parish, after only seven months there, the pastor thought it best for me to stop offering Sunday services, rather than try to address those expectations.

In late 2001, despite a busy ministry and being comfortable in the prison setting — imprisonment being familiar to me — I felt intense loneliness and emptiness. I compensated by spending more time and money in the gay social life. It took a critical incident at that point to keep me from full-blown depression arising from a sense of meaninglessness.

The 'Outing' — Part 2

My Sunday evening arrival at the Toronto airport on my way to Southdown was in sharp contrast to my Friday morning arrival at work at Headingley Correctional Centre. The Southdown chauffeur was no ordinary chauffeur. He was used to spotting people like me exiting the airport — apprehensive individuals looking for a white limo.

As I saw the limo, my mind flashed back to an inmate being released from prison to a very similar white limo. I remembered that the practice was done away with – limos are no longer allowed at Headingley. I shuddered. What would happen with my psychiatric evaluation here at Southdown? Would some of my practices be revoked as well?

"Are you Father Ray?" he stood by his car at the curb.

"Yes, I am."

"Welcome to Toronto," he replied. "Let me help you with your bags."

As he opened the back door of the car for me, I thought of Julia Roberts in the movie *Pretty Woman* sitting in the back seat of a luxurious limo.

The driver knew his passenger was uncomfortable, fearful, embarrassed. I had been given an ultimatum and he knew it. He had met many others like me and was experienced and well-trained in how to make me feel at ease.

We arrived after an hour of pleasantry while driving through the beautiful rolling farmlands north of Toronto. He talked about all the men and women he had made the same trip with and who had been so grateful for the experience I was about to have. His description of the centre and its setting were right on: they were both beautiful.

A matron came out to greet me and, after thanking the driver, I followed her inside. I felt as if I had left part of myself at the airport and was now on autopilot, leaving the control of events to others in what appeared to be a five-star resort.

I was immediately struck by how the other guests I encountered looked controlled, lacking warmth and conversation, as if they were from another world. After a coffee and an uncomfortable chitchat, I was led to my room and asked to complete a questionnaire. Obviously, life at Southdown was going to be quite regimented: breakfast at 8 a.m., which I could find by asking anyone I met; followed by my first appointment at 9 a.m. An entire week of appointments had been set up, with at least three different shrinks a day and a daily interview with my assigned primary doctor.

I filled out the questionnaire, which asked for detailed information about my childhood, adolescence, parents, family members, education, parish experiences, friends, etc, etc. Two hours later and very tired, I made for the bed, remembering to set my alarm.

At 7 a.m. I opened my blinds to a beautiful landscape of rolling hills, a manicured property, a pond, lawn chairs and park benches at various meditation points. I quickly got ready and said good morning to the first person I met.

"Where's the cafeteria?"

"Follow me."

The people at Southdown certainly knew how to treat men and women who were used to a privileged lifestyle, or perhaps thought they deserved it. There was no mistaking this was a five-star establishment, chefs and all.

The round cafeteria tables each held six people comfortably. "Good morning, may I join you?" I asked a group that had room for one more.

"By all means," came a southern accent from an elderly gentleman directly across the table.

We were considered patients, and were treated like patients and it quickly became apparent that most of my companions were under heavy medication, and had been for a long time.

"They decrease the dosage as you're feeling better," a sweet woman remarked.

I knew it; I could feel it in the air. Every day, I would be sitting with different priests and nuns from all over North America under obedience and filled with varying degrees of guilt, fear, anger, resentment, embarrassment, gratitude, and apprehension, yet hopeful about the future. Some were just grateful for time out. Many seemed reserved, distant, sad (some very sad), and others seemed right at home.

A large, quite impressive buffet was laid out for breakfast with a variety of cereals, juices, fruits, breads, eggs, bacon, ham, jams, coffees, teas, and water, with or without a wedge of lemon.

Lunch and supper were even more outstanding. We were graced with the presentation of variety, quantity and choice — five-star food — at every meal. General attentiveness was second perhaps only to that given folks in palliative care.

I was not medicated during my evaluation week and could feel the energy around me — it wasn't positive. Most of the others had been through their week of evaluation, had returned to their homes to discuss the results with their superiors and then been asked to come back to Southdown for treatment.

Treatment could last several months to as long as a year for depression, alcoholism, sexual misconduct and other questionable behaviours. I knew that it was costing my diocese a $1,000 a day to keep me there. This was serious business, the best food and shrinks that money could buy.

At the beginning of that week of assessment, my primary shrink asked, "Father Ray, what are you hoping to get from Southdown?"

"I hope to understand the reasons for the crises I've been having every five years."

"I don't think we're going to do that for you," he said. "But we'll give you tests to assess intellectual, pathological, psychological and health issues, and make suggestions to you and to your bishop."

I immediately began losing hope that something positive would come out of the experience.

The evaluation I was given at the end of the week stated that I had a sexual addiction because I refused to give up my active gay lifestyle. I'd told my shrink that he and his colleagues were ignorant of the normal psychology of a gay male. My remarks had the same effect on him as water on a duck's back.

The evaluation stated that I had a disorder referred to as a "narcissistic personality."

I was considered a liability to the church because I was not accepting celibacy, and could implicate the church in further accusations and possible lawsuits.

They concluded I couldn't be rehabilitated, nor reprogrammed, as I had interpreted it, back into a celibate, clerical box so that I wouldn't cause any more waves, which is also my interpretation.

That evening, as I walked in the woods along the property, I prayed, "Dear God, speak to me through my bishop," which he wasted no time in doing.

Even after returning from Southdown, I couldn't recognize the signs that the priesthood was not a healthy lifestyle for me as a gay male. I was still prepared to go along with anything the bishop asked of me to protect myself, safeguard my own security, and get him off my back. But the bishop had already made up his mind. With the assessment and support from Southdown stating that rehabilitation was unlikely, I had to be cut loose.

Within ten minutes of calling me into his office, the bishop said, "Ray, we have come to a crossroads. Since Southdown says you can't be rehabilitated, I'm removing your faculties."

This meant he was revoking my authorization to function as a priest,

He also suggested that I request laicization. This means the Pope revokes my clerical status which also removes any legal ties with the diocese.

"I'm no longer going to support you as a chaplain," he added. "You'll need to find employment elsewhere."

Then, in a gesture of fraternal and collegial affection, he gave me a hug, which felt like it was a whole minute long, and reminded me of a certain Judas incident. Then I was asked to leave. I'll never forget the feeling that came over me as I walked out — a sense of freedom — though I didn't understand why at the time.

The following day, I met with the superintendent at Headingley and told him what had happened and about the assessment.

"My faculties have been removed," I said.

"Oh... does that mean you're now brain dead?" he smirked.

After a needed laugh, he assured me of his support and told me I was appreciated and that a two-year term position had just come up, which I qualified for and would give me time to make my transition. Not only was God guiding and protecting me, he was using a prison to keep me safe.

The bishop quickly removed my benefits and privileges and offered me $25,000 to help with my transition, and for the 24 years I had given to the diocese. His assistant had mentioned on a few occasions that the diocese wanted to offer me the money as a matter of justice.

Shortly afterwards, I went on a weekend workshop given by O'Murchu on the topic of his book *Reclaiming Spirituality*. The term "the disfunctionate church" was used but I never felt comfortable with it because it painted everyone in the church with the same brush. O'Murehu said the church hierarchy consisted of only about one percent of the whole church while the faithful and the laity made up the remaining ninety-nine percent.

That insight prepared me for my next workshop, in June 2002, which was on domestic abuse. I attended along with a few correctional officers from the Domestic Abuse Unit at Headingley. As I listened, I could relate a lot of what was said to the relationship I'd had with my mother, and with the hierarchy of the church — that one percent who have all the power and control and who make the final decisions on all matters.

When, as a child and later as a priest, I had believed I was the problem because I didn't fit in, that I wasn't good enough, I always felt like a helpless victim, filled with fear and vulnerability. I was being emotionally abused because I didn't feel free to be myself, to know and express myself. I also feared leaving the church because I thought I would lose respect, my pension, a secured retirement with benefits, and the friends I had as a priest. The losses seemed to outweigh the benefits of freedom and peace of mind.

I not only learned a great deal through those workshops but I also acquired a language that facilitated my understanding of all that I had mistakenly hoped to get at Southdown. I understood why I hadn't fit in with the institution — I was gay!

I understood why, like clockwork, I had fallen into a crisis every few years — my body was trying to tell me it couldn't take the pain of being so alone!

I understood why I felt so lonely and trapped — the church institution would never accept me as an active gay male and would never allow me to have a significant other in my life as a priest!

And I understood why, once out of the priesthood, I felt free!

The attitude and mentality in a prison either makes or breaks a person. At Headingley, I became less sensitive to the comments and attitudes of others. A few officers, who offered me the opportunity to debrief with them during my transition, often asked, "Father Ray, will you be mentioning me in your book?"

I would smile and reply, "You'll be happier if I don't."

The transition was a time of things coming to a head, of identifying with differing points of view and spiritualities and of doing more meaningful work inside. As many people are rejected by society, I was rejected by the Catholic institution. But in the prison environment, outside of the church and surrounded by beautiful trees and nature, my relationship with God flourished... the prison set me free!

I respect those who continue to find fulfillment and spiritual support in their particular denomination, along with a profound feeling of freedom. I respect the ministers who serve their communities with devotion, respect and a sense of mission and vision.

3

GRATITUDE

My Spirituality

My spirituality used to be within a religious context that included words such as guilt, sinful, immoral, perverse, and unnatural. These words had me living a life of ambiguity. I could never reconcile that God was a God of unconditional love while being taught that I was going against His plan of creation by being gay and living a sinful life because of my sexuality and erotic fantasies.

In order to live a normal gay life with a God of unconditional love, I needed a spirituality outside the particular religious box that I'd been born into.

Within the formal church, words such as obedience, penance, infallibility, celibacy, submission, abstinence, excommunication, annulment and heresy, to name just a few, are needed to maintain power and control. Eventually these became unacceptable to me. The language of faith, values and beliefs is expressed in different ways by other religions and forms of spirituality and, for me, it is not and never was about which is better. It's about the need to respect, and to have the right to choose freely according to one's conscience.

My experiences have taught me that while maintaining steadfastness to my own path to truth, I need to respect all other paths to that same truth, which is that love is all, irrespective of religion, culture, colour or creed.

Just the notion of God conjures up all kinds of images and, for many, these images are quite negative. But many of us believe that

God uses events and individuals in our lives to reach our hearts and remind us to continue to have faith and hope. We blame God less by not using phrases such as "the will of God" or "an act of God." Instead we need only ask God to help us through the natural events in our lives.

The spiritual revival that has been taking place in recent years has offered me an image of God that's more believable, especially as a gay person. This image has helped me connect more easily with nature and with others who make up my life.

In 2005, I experienced a paradigm shift from an image of God as father to an image of God as one divine energy, one infinite presence outside a religious box — and for this, I owe eternal gratitude to my brother Gaetan. My brother always had a dislike for and rebelled against two institutions: school and church. For him, they were truly necessary evils.

Unknown to me in 2005, Gaetan had been engrossed in the writings of Dr. Wayne W. Dyer, particularly his book *The Power of Intention*. So, when he called me for information about the spiritual group that our younger sister belonged to, "The Army of Mary," he assumed that I, his religious brother, could shed some light on Denise's very religious spirituality.

For our sister and her family, devotion to Mary brings them into a community of faith with strong spiritual friends, which enriches their lives and devotion to God. Though it's not a form of spirituality that Gaetan and I, nor our other sister, follow, it's one that we respect as being meaningful for Denise and her family.

When Gaetan called to gain some insight from me, he was surprised to discover my own spiritual paradigm had shifted. As he spoke of his new-found spirituality, I was hearing a spiritual language that I could relate to, which was especially surprising coming from this unexpected messenger.

As I worked on moving forward throughout 2005 and 2006, Gaetan and I kept in close contact, giving each other spiritual support and encouragement. God does, indeed, work in mysterious ways.

There's a saying that when the student is ready, the master appears and events are presented that open our minds to what we need. In July, 2006, while vacationing in Toronto, a friend invited me to attend the Unity Church there. The theme that Sunday was "Always look on the bright side of things" and, in keeping with that theme, though I don't think it was his intention; he was excited about introducing me to a book that he was reading, *You Can Heal Your Life*, by Louise L. Hay.

The following month, I was hired as a spiritual counsellor at a local health centre. I decided to leave the prison after my two-year term was completed. While it had afforded me freedom, my freedom now was in seeing where my new language of spirituality would lead me. At the health centre I worked with four alternative healers. I was so impressed with Hay's book that I began recommending it to my clients and using it as my own spiritual reading.

Within a few weeks, I saw the film *What the Bleep!? Down the Rabbit Hole*, which deals with quantum physics. I was so surprised to hear others speak my spiritual language that I went back to see the film another few times that same weekend.

Then, from the Universe, my sister Denise sent me the book and DVD called *The Secret*, about the law of attraction. I watched that DVD over and over again.

Shortly after that, she put the icing on the cake by mailing me Eckhart Tolle's book *A New Earth*. It deals with awakening to your life's purpose and is endorsed by Oprah Winfrey.

These spiritual writers led me to the language of my spirituality today, a spirituality in which I refer to God as Divine Energy, Infinite Presence. Others refer to the same God as Lord, Father, Abba, Allah, Krishna, Yahweh, Creator, Manitou, Higher Power, Mother Earth, Divine Source, etc.

For me, and many others, spirituality has become being in a harmonious relationship with myself — body, mind and spirit — as well as with others, and with God, however we might understand God to be.

To have this harmony and balance within myself, I first need to be conscious of what is taking place in my life, in my body, mind and spirit in the now, as Eckhart Tolle would say — and be able to interpret, learn from, and be grateful for the experiences, no matter how difficult or challenging they may be.

When we are self-aware, we're better able to connect to our conscience. We know something is right when our conscience is clear, which is why we need to learn to listen to and trust its voice. My conscience accepts my orientation and lifestyle as normal and fulfilling, whereas to a religious person, such a lifestyle might be seen as unnatural and perverse.

We must believe what our consciences and gut feelings tell us, and be responsible for our choices. Only then can we become the unique persons we are called to be, whether we are to live for a few or many years.

To have harmony and balance with others, we must have respect, love, tolerance and honesty. These allow us to share our truths while respecting the choices and beliefs of others, thereby drawing into our lives the people and events that our spirit-energy attracts.

On February 28, 2004, I saw a play entitled *Liar*, by Brian Drader, an actor, writer and dramatist who made Winnipeg his home. I related to many statements he made in speaking about one of the main characters in the play.

I too, "had lived (almost) entirely outside of the box, and had defied conventional categorization."

I too, "could be all things..." (a good priest, a sexually active man, a relative and an acquaintance) "except possibly myself" (a compassionate, loving, gay man).

To most people who knew and worked with me, I too was "the mysterious stranger, the loner."

Brian also wrote that "intimacy and honesty need to be linked." When I finally realized the truth of that statement, I began experiencing both honesty and intimacy.

Indeed, as Brian said, "I found myself in a very different place," experiencing harmony and balance within myself, among my body, mind and spirit, and having learned a very different lesson — to let go and let God by living one day at a time — as prescribed in AA and other 12-step programs.

And to have harmony and balance with God, we are called to have daily gratitude and trust in the process of life, and to rest easy in knowing that our prayers are being answered by Infinite Intelligence. I believe that my spirit will continue to learn lessons from experiences, to become ready to be one with its source, its God.

Some, like author/photographer Tom Bianchi, look for a language for happiness outside the language of religion, of having the pieces but not the understanding needed to put them together. Having harmony and balance within ourselves and between ourselves and our Higher Power will bring about what many are searching for –- happiness and inner peace.

Beyond reconciliation

My sister Carole, whose input and support has been a godsend, raised an important, though not surprising question: "Ray, why would God call you to be a priest knowing you're gay?" Quite a loaded question!

A similar question is asked of married men who, after twenty, even forty years of marriage, come out — with all the shock and scandal that such an announcement always creates. But that same affirmation from a priest seems more sinister and deceitful to everyone — except to God and the priest himself.

However, while coming out was not a sinister and deceitful revelation to me, nor to God, in order to move on in my spiritual life and gain balance and harmony, I had some work to do:

1. ...on myself, because I had to accept that for my entire life, in keeping my secret to myself, I hadn't been honest

2. ...on my relationships with others, because I had to address the whole difficult issue of reconciliation

3. ...on my relationship with God — I had to move my outlook and attitude to a place of gratitude for my journey

From the beginning. I hadn't been honest with myself, nor encouraged to be. I was raised in a devout Roman Catholic home in which God was seen as up in heaven and was only happy with me when I was an obedient, good boy, like the one spoken of in *The Best Little Boy in the World* by John Reid, alias Andrew Tobias.

As a boy, I was very sensitive and knew early on that there was something different about me. Fearing rejection by my parents, I kept my secret with God.

As an adolescent, my emerging sexuality and attraction to males led to issues of acceptance, fear of being discovered and a need for fantasies and masturbation. As well, I was filled with worry about my future and guilt for not being as good a boy as others thought I was.

My parents were deeply concerned about each of their children, but our basic needs for love, affection, affirmation and unconditional acceptance were experienced and interpreted differently by each of us. At the time, we were too young to understand what was happening and didn't have a language with which to articulate it.

As adults who survived the experience, we find ourselves almost estranged from one another, not having the closeness we experienced as children. When we meet again, it won't be to hash over the past because our experiences of it were so different for each of us. Instead, it's my hope that we'll meet each other in the moment, the now, and move beyond past hurts.

Throughout my adult life, each personal crisis affected my physical well-being and, I believe, always had its roots in suppressing my sexuality. My body was trying to make me reflect on what was happening, to force me to make different choices to find peace and no longer feel so alone in the midst of so many people and so much activity. I was annoyed with authority, those to whom I had promised loyalty and obedience. I was searching for a place of belonging and my symptoms — anger, annoyance and episodes of health problems — were my first sense of the price I would pay until I found that place.

During the transition to honesty with myself, I questioned every aspect of my life and identified with different points of view and spiritualties. Finally, I no longer saw rejection as negative, neither the church's rejection of me, nor my rejection of some of the beliefs for which it stood. The mini-transitions along the way were part of the process of letting go, but still included intense emotion and loneliness.

In each transition, two things happened within me: I was told that it was no longer enough to be a priest and also gay; and I was offered an opportunity to clear the decks and be honest, particularly with myself.

In 1990, when my shrink asked me if I loved myself, I was dumbfounded because it was difficult to love the image that others had of me, and which I somehow knew wasn't really me. I needed to be healthy within myself — body, mind and spirit — in order to take care of myself.

With low self-esteem, I had been living my life in survival mode, doing everything I could to meet the expectations of others. I wasn't thinking of self-care.

At minor seminary, which was the beginning of my spiritual formation into the priesthood, I did gain a measure of acceptance and freedom as I became an adult and an individual with some sense of self. Being in the company of so many other men, it was also a time of homo-eroticism during which I felt, even more strongly, the need to protect my secret from others in order to remain accepted, even if it meant being dishonest with everyone.

Meanwhile, the Institute Voluntas Dei was giving me a spirituality through the 5-5-5, and through my walks in the woods, a new awareness that my relationship with God and a sense of God's presence could exist outside of the institution of the church.

Later, I began disliking some of the things I was asking of my parishioners because I no longer believed what I was preaching. I was living with ambiguity but was not comfortable with the idea of accepting that ambiguity.

More recently, at a penitential service in which I was assisting a few priests in hearing individual confessions for a parish community, an elderly man sat in a chair facing me. He was obviously uncomfortable and quite upset about what he wanted to say. He told me that he was concerned about having masturbated a few times during the previous week. He was obviously sorry for committing what he perceived to be a serious sin when, in reality, he was deeply missing his wife, who had recently died.

His sad confession was one of the many experiences that finally brought me to the realization that I had had enough. I no longer wanted to listen to the guilt and shame that so many good people felt trapped within, particularly when I knew that by doing so I was enabling them to remain trapped.

At that same service, with a line of people waiting to confess such sins as having forgotten to say their morning or night prayers, or having missed mass, there was no time to reassure the widower that what he had been doing was not wrong, nor displeasing to God. In fact, I wondered whether I should congratulate him on still being sexually alive, or to merely forgive him for his sinful acts. I opted for forgiveness and asked God to forgive me.

I had often been reminded by bishops to keep my personal opinions to myself, to watch what I said and not cause waves. There were consequences for anyone expressing an opinion outside of company policy and without permission.

I met many wonderful people during my ministry and my greatest regret is not having been honest with them about myself. In the book *Intimacy*, Henri Nouwen writes that the more of us we deny, repress and stifle in a relationship, the more partial, limited and impoverished the relationship will be.

In every parish there must have been other men and women who carried the same secret as me, feeling they had to get married because, like Henri Nouwen and me, they feared rejection and the consequences of being openly gay or bisexual. Though I tried, my loneliness couldn't be alleviated by putting on clerical clothing; only through the company of others like myself, within a community in which I felt I belonged, could I hope for peace. What I didn't fully realize was the price I'd have to pay for claiming my freedom.

I had always hoped that gay priests would be accepted by the church hierarchy but the expression, "Hell would freeze over first," applies here. In 2002, the silencing by the church of a priest and a nun, who were both involved in the gay movement, was a foreshadowing event for me.

With people in the gay community mentoring me, I was not only able to come out, but to burst out! My lifestyle was more open and obsessive. And then, having lived outside the box of dogmas, rules, regulations and labels, I came to understand and accept that I no longer fit into communities that judged me.

I had invested a great deal of myself in my role as a priest — 25 years of my life. I lost many contacts and had to learn how to cope with the ensuing isolation and alienation, not only of leaving the priesthood, but also of preparing myself to be known as a gay person. This was the price to pay for "owning my truth," as Ellen DeGeneres calls it.

After spending so many years studying to become a priest, and having been encouraged to feel that I had chosen, and reached, the ultimate vocation, my experiences, social context, language, values, beliefs, faith, identity and energy were all within a very religious context. The Catholic Church invested a great deal of money and time to form me, and it didn't appreciate my stepping out of the program. A great deal time and energy was put into trying to keep me content and holding to the party line. And, indeed, I felt a sense of responsibility to Mother Church and to all who had helped me along the way. I didn't want to let them down. But when I did finally step out of line, I had to either get reprogrammed or be honest with myself and move on. I moved on!

Reconciliation with others hasn't been possible in every case, nor even of importance in some cases, though it certainly has been important in the process of my learning to own my truth. Many people have been significant in my life but I accept that it may not be possible for all of them to accept me for who I am, nor should they have to. But I am no longer alone; members of my current extended family all fly the same rainbow flag and do so with pride and gratitude to God.

I'd like my sister Carole to know that I believe God spared my life in the 60s by leading me into the priesthood. Had I come out back then, rejection by our family and my friends might have caused me to take my own life or, entering the sexual promiscuity of that era, I most likely would have been among those who have since died of AIDS.

Though church institutions no longer meet my spiritual needs, I have moved beyond reconciliation to a spirituality and faith outside the institution. I have learned that, yes, God is certainly within institutions, but He is also beyond institutions and can't be controlled, manipulated, nor copyrighted.

My meditations, Tai Chi, walks in the woods and gay spirituality sharing groups have become my connection with God. With our God-given gifts and the spiritual and social support of whatever community we might belong to, God calls each of us to celebrate life with hope and pride.

I've always had a strong love of God, a caring spirit, and the creative flare and sense of humour that have kept me strong and likeable. God, the One Divine Energy, One Infinite Presence, has used my gifts in the service of many.

I believe men who are in committed relationships with women, yet frequent gay bath houses for physical intimacy, are seeking out others who have the same secret. No one, other than another kindred spirit, can understand this need, and only another kindred spirit who has had his secret disclosed, can understand with empathy the pain that his secret is causing, or will cause everyone in his life, especially himself.

Reconciliation with others, as much as it's possible, is also desirable. However, what's important is that each of us finds practices, whether religious or not, that express our spirituality, free our consciences and allow us to be honest and intimate. I now see my spiritual journey, not as the price I've paid, but rather as the grace I've been given to live it out.

Then there's my relationship with God. During the time between minor seminary and major seminary, I was an introvert, experiencing the world while still suppressing my sexuality, questioning my calling and trying to figure out how God fit into my life.

During my pastoral experience in the Arctic, I felt God's presence in the wild nature of the north, just as I had found Him in the woods of the south. I gained a sense of freedom from authority in such life experiences while searching for a place in which I could be myself.

In major seminary, I was filled with anxiety and doubts around the notion of being "in" the world but not "of" it. My relationship with God existed in rituals and I felt uncomfortable with church dictates that began with, "It is the will of God that...." or "God says..."

Identifying with causes and alternate spiritualties gave me freedom from the status quo of the church culture. But behind all my causes were the overriding issues of acceptance as a gay person, and how to relate to my place within the church. Through causes, my relationship with God was redefined outside the institution of the church as I became more honest in owning my own truth.

To move on and have harmony and balance in my relationship with my Higher Power, I accepted addressing God as Divine Energy, Infinite Presence. I am now truly grateful for the gift of this journey that has been my life. It has led to my current spiritual beliefs and work as a spiritual counsellor which offer me the opportunity of encouraging and creating wider acceptance and tolerance.

I am grateful for the relationships I've had with others because none of my life would have happened as it has without them. If not for the prison incident and the people involved, for example, I might still be a priest today, although, in the end, not really functioning as one.

My secret with God went on for years and accentuated feelings of being alone, but it also made me sensitive to issues of injustice within a minority group.

I'm so grateful for the experience of feeling God's daily presence and for the necessary lessons of faith and courage in my spiritual journey.

And I am extremely grateful to the Roman Catholic Church for the education it afforded me, for the formation of my spirituality, for the numerous beautiful people I have met and served and the for the fraternity I've had with so many gifted, spiritual men and women. Though there may not be reconciliation with this community that can't accept me for who I am and how I live, I remain grateful. I've moved beyond reconciliation.

I've moved beyond the religiosity of the denomination that I lived in and served for most of my life, with its dogmas, expectations and rituals. I left, not with anger, but with disappointment and a profound feeling of freedom.

CONCLUSION

The Fish Bowl:

Jimmy had four pet goldfish that his parents bought him for his ninth birthday. Every night before he went to bed, he would watch the delicate, orange-coloured fish swim round and round in the small glass bowl.

One day, Jimmy noticed that the water in the bowl looked kind of cloudy and the glass was covered with a light film. Jimmy's mom explained to him that what he saw was natural and that the goldfish bowl just needed to be cleaned.

Jimmy knew how to clean the bowl. He had seen his friend Howie do it. He filled up his bathtub with water and put his hand in it to ensure it was the same temperature as the water in the bowl. Then he gently lowered the bowl into the tub until the four goldfish swam out of it and into the tub, where they waited for the housecleaning to be completed.

Later, as Jimmy knelt by the bathtub to retrieve his goldfish, he saw a strange sight. Even though the bathtub was over four feet long and three feet wide, the four goldfish were swimming round and round in a tiny circle, right where Jimmy had originally placed them.

"Mom," yelled Jimmy, "come and look at the goldfish."

Jimmy's mom came into the bathroom to see what all the fuss was about.

"Why are the fish swimming in a little circle when they have a whole tub?"

Jimmy's mom smiled at her son, "Because they don't know they're in the tub. They think they're still at home in their tiny glass bowl. That's what they're used to."

We're often not that different from Jimmy's goldfish. Even when we're offered an opportunity to change and grow, we decide, instead, to remain living the way we have been, within the same little boundaries, swimming in our same little circles. We choose the familiar over the unfamiliar, the old over the new. We get attached to staying in our comfort zone and we resist taking risks and flowing with the changes that would force us to face the unknown.

And, sometimes, even when life makes those changes for us, like those goldfish, we stubbornly try to hang onto our old realities and fight the transformation that's already taking place.

Living in a fish bowl offered me security and safety, but I wasn't happy because I wasn't free. My experience had been that of an emotionally abused person who lived under the power and control of others. That experience taught me how to survive and how to relate to others through the same defence mechanisms that were used on me.

Being treated like a child or an object was minimized by my abusers as being less serious than what I claimed. Having adults in my life denying they had said a certain thing resulted in my refusing to admit to things that I had said and done ... with a free conscience. I lived according to the example that was shown me.

As a child and teen, I was told what to believe and I had to go along with it or be rejected. I felt helpless because I didn't know who to talk to, and I was made to believe that there was something wrong with me and/or I was just being difficult, again.

I had my parents' religion and mirrored their involvement in their traditions when I was growing up. The rituals of those traditions became part of our family's culture, sometimes with symbols, such as our family Bible and maintaining burial plots. We learned certain hymns, worship styles, ideas, role models and lifestyles.

Being accepted into the seminary seemed a natural fit for me. I was a good person, obedient, submissive, religious and I enjoyed learning and studying. However, in her book, *The Drama of the Gifted Child*, Alice Miller writes: "If both spiritual hunger and dependency on human loving are denied or rejected, the only thing left is narcissism."

During my first three years of seminary study I was allowed to return home for Christmas, Easter and summer. If I didn't have a summer job, the staff would find one for me on campus. While away from home, I was able to express myself more; I became more confident and a freer thinker.

I lived in a fishbowl for the first fifty-eight years of my life. During that time, I doubted my own experiences and lived the expectations of others.

Abuse can be defined as a union based on one person having all the power and control. I learned how to be obedient to the expectations of others, and I was well-disposed to having the power and control wielded by my mother passed on to an institution that really knew how to use it as well.

Although I had knowledge about who I was and what my personality traits were, I didn't have a heartfelt experience of my own feelings and emotions because I wasn't living in freedom. My knowledge couldn't be integrated into a heartfelt, passionate experience.

My relationships were superficial, since I hadn't attained an intimacy within myself that would allow me to be honest with myself, let alone with others. I was in denial of what was happening to me, and fearful of being rejected. That was my experience as an emotionally abused person. I've struggled with internal confusion most of my life. I was made to believe that my thoughts and perceptions were wrong because others didn't agree, or because institutions taught something different. As a child, I doubted my tendency for questioning everything. As a teen, I doubted my experience of sexual fantasies and desires. As a priest, I doubted my experience of being misunderstood, of being a free thinker. Why?

From their experience as a victim, an emotionally abused person can't relate to words such as freedom, vitality, intimacy, certainty, confidence, self-respect, harmony, true self, spontaneity, honesty and integration. Abused people are constantly second-guessing themselves, being belittled, being made to feel they are wrong and inferior.

In 2002, when I attended a workshop on domestic abuse, everything being said about an abused person applied to me. For the first time in my life, I had words that related to my experiences, to my feelings and my emotions as a child and as a priest.

For the first time, I knew why I hadn't been happy. I could relate a lot of what was being said to my own relationship with my mother, but the most striking revelation was yet to come. The insight I gained from that workshop gave me the language I needed to understand why it would be so difficult for me to leave my emotionally abusive situation, and why I felt so ambivalent about so many things.

I needed to know that I was not defined by my experience of abuse. Through the language of domestic abuse, I began to recognize who I was dealing with. It became clear that the hierarchy (the one percent) had use of me as long as I was kept in line. Step outside their boundaries and I would quickly be put back in my place, even if it took trying to reprogram me to do so.

As an emotionally abused person, my need was to understand the trauma of abuse that I experienced during my life. I needed to realize that I couldn't be blamed and held responsible for the expectations others had of me. I was not a bad priest, and I could have been happier with the parishioners had I been treated like an adult and not as a child making waves. Being treated like a child made me aware that my unhappiness had more to do with a dissatisfied abuser and the institution than it did with my being unfaithful to the message of Jesus.

I struggled with worrying what others would think and say if they knew about my sexual orientation, about how I was treated as a priest and about what I no longer believed. I struggled with the state of guilt and shame that I kept my parishioners in while not believing much of what I was being asked to preach. I stayed in the clerical subculture hoping that the situation would get better ... and out of a sense of responsibility.

As I pondered leaving, I feared the unknown, not knowing what else to do, the loss of community, a lack of money, not wanting to let others down and what others would think.

I was always very fortunate in the resources I had outside of myself. During my studies in 1995 in pastoral counselling, I was able to articulate my spiritual questions. My mentors gave encouragement and support as I spoke about my desire to move beyond religiosity to spirituality. O'Murchu's book, *Reclaiming Spirituality*, has since given me the language I needed to articulate my spiritual experience.

From 2002 to 2004, I was grateful for the resources that were already in place for me, and for those that the correctional institution offered. Those resources allowed for the end to the cycle of abuse that I had been experiencing, not at the hands of the Catholic Church, which is ninety-nine percent faithful people, but rather by the one percent.

Within the institution, I had everything I needed to live — housing, food, insurance, health benefits, a pension, resources of every kind, educational opportunities, access to professionals and tips/stipends on the side. Three days after I was asked to leave, I lost all of those perks, except for my vehicle, which was my own.

If you don't have family or friends who can help you financially, or if you haven't had the opportunity to save some money, you have a hurdle to get over. Your diocese may, out of a sense of justice, offer you some money to get you on your feet. But this donation won't be an unconditional gift. You might have to sign a waiver of silence in order to make sure you don't write about your experiences — another way of maintaining control over you, even when justice and compassion should be offered instead.

Being asked to leave provided a sense of freedom as I left the bishop's office for the last time. But still, to survive such a shock to my system, I needed to have a number of resources in place, or the shock would have immobilized me.

Since I had been controlled from the outside by fear and guilt, my religious life isolated me from free thinkers who were seen as dissenters. I needed a number of things:

- Information about what was available outside of my present situation, and about what to anticipate before, during and after leaving
- The affection, encouragement, support and time of friends, family and acquaintances... at least one other person who would be a positive support so I wouldn't feel alone, as I had often felt in the past.
- Support groups and a counsellor to mentor me through the transition
- Legal advice, financial assistance, material assets
- A safe place to live
- To continue to take care of my physical, mental and spiritual health
- The commitment and belief that I could make the transition and form a concrete plan of action that would give me affirmation and support to go through with it

In seeking advice and counselling, I needed to understand the trauma of abuse and the psychological impact of having been abused. I needed to feel that I wasn't being blamed, pathologized, judged, nor held responsible. I needed someone to understand the difficulty of leaving and the societal sanctions against it; to understand my ambivalence and that I am not defined by my experience of abuse.

I couldn't have left without having my own apartment, another job, support from management, or emotional and psychological support from the staff. I couldn't have moved on without friends offering me empathy, support, information, outside help, sensitivity, confidence, compassion, non-judgement, people to talk with or without the re-education in clinical counselling that offered me a different perspective.

And I couldn't have left without outside help from medical, financial, legal and spiritual counselling.

The hierarchy maintains strong control over its codependent priests by making sure they have just enough money to exist. I was made to believe that I was at the service of the Church and God and, like Jesus, was to have no spare change.

Without the resources in place, I wouldn't have been able to make the transition, and would've subjected myself to a continuing abusive relationship (co-dependency). The one percent (the hierarchy) counts us fearing for our security and having self-doubt to prevent us from moving on.

Luckily, the answers to all my needs fell into place. Otherwise separation would have been even more traumatic because an abuser always enforces a separation by totally withdrawing compassion and further contact. But with all my needs being met in a fashion, the separation became freeing. Without that freedom, one remains abused, fearful and in a constant state of vulnerability. It was only when I claimed my freedom, that I could see my life from a different perspective, and with hope.

As a child, I had to be an obedient boy, and then an obedient priest. I knew what others expected of me and I knew my boundaries. I learned how to live in a fish bowl but I wasn't happy. Even though others around me were kind to me and very accommodating, they could sense I wasn't happy, but they didn't understand why... nor did I.

In the priesthood, if you think for yourself and follow your own conscience, you're considered to be stepping out of line. If you speak your opinions out loud, you're considered a dissenter. If you swim outside the group, you're considered disloyal.

Those of us who've been in an abusive relationship can relate to the fish in the fishbowl story. Although there was an entire world outside of our own, we felt secure and safe swimming in our small circle. We would've been fearful of swimming outside our group.

No one else seemed to be venturing forth… and what if we couldn't get back into the group? What would become of us?

In thinking about venturing beyond the group boundaries you become a thinker, a dissenter, and you become politically dangerous, even though, in most other social contexts, dissent is seen as a sign of democracy and a challenge to change; an evolution.

Today, the media are helping us to have a voice, and parishioners who themselves may be living in abusive situations, are seeing the signs of abuse and are able to articulate their experience. They are saying, "Enough!"

Many abused people will relate to the price I had to pay to get my freedom. I had invested a great deal of myself into my role as a priest — twenty-five years of my life! Upon leaving, I lost many contacts, and I had to learn how to cope with the ensuing isolation and alienation, not only of leaving the priesthood, but also of preparing myself to be known as a gay person.

It's said that an addiction will end only when the person reaches rock bottom. I learned how to feel helpless because I always thought that I had no choices in my life, although I did. This inability to make choices affected my self-esteem, perceptions and behaviours.

Being unable to see the effect that the use of power and control, exercised by both my mother and the one percent, was having on me at the time, I felt trapped into a life of co-dependency, guilt, shame, fear and perfectionism. Not having anyone to help me to see the situation also contributed to my feeling helpless. Recovery requires a fundamental choice: addiction or wholeness.

Whatever the choices we have to make in our lives, they'll probably involve some sort of price being paid. It was when I began to see the signs of my abuse that I understood what my body had been trying to tell me every time I became ill, about every five years.

I had lived a life of security and isolation under the control of an institution that I had always thought was going to be there for me, no matter what.

A new era is upon us in which people are no longer accepting control by guilt, shame and intimidation.

Society has evolved, is more educated, less naïve, more tolerant, and though less religious, more spiritually conscious. And the hierarchy (the one percent) is about to be challenged by this society, which won't be tolerant of blind obedience and abuse of any kind, neither in the name of God, nor of Mother Church.

Concerning religion, some say it's only a matter of time until things rebound. Others speak of a pendulum-like swing. Some believe that religion is unlikely to be replaced by secular substitutes. Some believe that new religious groups will arise in response to the core questions of existence, death, tragedy, obligation and love. Some believe that this accounts for the emergence of charismatic and evangelical groups.

Also, trying to help us understand the meaning of life is the New Age Movement, which is often spoken about along with other fringe activities like transcendental meditation, astrology, tarot cards, reincarnation, out-of-body experiences, and dream analysis.

However, the New Age Movement has become a significant spiritual movement. It has focused on the tapping of one's potential, personal spirituality, the spirit world, the oneness of creation, the limitless potential of humanity, and possibility of transforming the self and today's world into a better one.

That the hierarch (the one percent) is so fearful and defensive about the New Age Movement is understandable. It threatens the status quo and the income of orthodox religious groups and can't be contained in a box. It's often spoken of out of fear, self-righteousness, lack of tolerance, and insecurity.

As people move on in their social, political, economic and cultural lives, they also move on in their spiritual lives. They leave behind the politics of denominational concerns about membership, dogma, and self-righteousness.

Change often puts things into perspective and cleanses the soul.

People are at peace with their educated consciences as they search for forms and expressions of spirituality that connect their lives more closely within themselves, with others, and with the God of their understanding.

Many are searching for forms and expressions of spirituality that will enable them to articulate their personal experience and help them connect their lives more closely. For some, that means joining another denomination or religion. For others, it means supplementing their present faith experience with New Age spirituality, creation spirituality or native spirituality.

It's known that the world can articulate itself through the body. This notion can help to explain what is sometimes called the sixth sense or the ability to acquire knowledge about a person or an event without the use of ordinary means of perception. It seems to imply some kind of underlying unity in creation whereby particular items of information can occasionally be deciphered by people with the right kind of psychic sensitivity. Psychologists refer to this as clairvoyance, ascetical theology talks of infused knowledge, and Hinduism refers to subtle consciousness.

I know what it feels like to go through experiences without a language to express feelings and emotions; to be treated as an object, programmed to obey and not to question; to be labelled as disobedient and yet know that you're a good person who has the respect and love of others, and of God. To be made to feel guilty for not fitting in, for wanting to do your own thing, and hurting the others around you who want you to be accepted by the institution, and in turn, by God.

Jesus was for people of all faiths and spiritualties, not to convince them to change their faith, but to live it out in a more harmonious and healthy way.

In asking us to "love God with our whole heart, mind and soul, and our neighbour as ourselves," Jesus was saying that we must love ourselves before we can love anyone else. And in loving our neighbour, we show our love of God by being in healthy relationships, which he created us to be in.

There's no place for self-righteous claims on the truth in today's multi-cultural world. Even when religious groups stick to religion, they may not have a lot of freedom to be very assertive. Academics have legitimized the "everything is relative" idea. Religious groups are called upon to recognize that ours is now a multi-faith world. The principles of tolerance and acceptance are the norm. There is little room or appreciation for competition. If a variety of lifestyles, moralities, and religions are all to have a place under one societal roof, each must be seen as a valid option for all.

Truth has to be seen in terms of personal preference. A society that is multi-cultural can't permit proponents of one cultural style or sexual orientation, abortion view or world view to impose its positions, its truths on others. The diplomatic way to resolve the problem of diverse outlooks is to decree that they're all relative.

My last bishop saw that I didn't fit in, and that I was a liability to him and his institution. By sending me to Southdown, his suspicions were confirmed, which justified his getting rid of me. That experience was not the tragedy I had feared it would be. On the contrary, it was a catalyst in giving me the freedom for which I longed. I was able to ask my questions, to have my experiences validated and to pursue my spiritual journey.

A REFLECTION

The arts and my human experiences have taught me in a way that has been captivating and memorable. I enjoy visual stimulation and learning through seeing. I believe our brains, when taking in new visual stimuli often improve the learning for many of us.

The movie Philomena was one such visual learning experience for me. It's the true story of a mother's search for her lost son, based on the celebrated book by Martin Sixsmith, *The Lost Child of Philomena Lee*, published in 2009. The movie serves as an excellent visual example of what I refer to as moving beyond reconciliation.

When she got pregnant as a teenager in 1950s Ireland, Philomena was sent to the convent of Roscrea to be looked after. She was what the Catholic hierarchy would call a fallen woman (pregnant and unwed). That meant the nuns would serve as enablers by selling the newborn children for adoption in America. The nuns' actions were blessed by the Catholic Institution because the mothers were seen as having been sinful, and if they were seen that way by the church, they would be seen that way by God also.

Philomena spent the next fifty years searching in vain for her son. Then she met Martin Sixsmith, a world-weary political journalist who was intrigued by her story. Critics call the film a compelling narrative of human love and loss, and ultimately a celebration of life — true enough, but I see it as much more than that. For me, Philomena is a perfect example of someone who moved beyond reconciliation.

Despite all the denials and the lies from the nuns and the years of anguish they had caused Philomena, she's able to say, "Enough!"

and walk out of the church. She realized that the nuns did what they felt was right, and being angry at them would only fill her with resentment and bitterness; it wouldn't bring her son back to her. She was moving beyond reconciliation, which was impossible.

Not all nuns were created equal, of course. One day, a young nun gives Philomena a photo of her son, which she had stolen from the files. She would have been seriously disciplined for that, and might have been, since she was later transferred from that convent.

Towards the end of the movie, Philomena and Martin confront the aged nun who had played a big part in separating her from her son. The nun looks at Philomena with the same distain and self-righteousness that filled her when they were much younger. Philomena looks at her and says, "I just want you to know that I forgive you."

The old nun, still filled with the same denial and venom, responds that she has nothing to be forgiven for and that she has only God to answer to, since she was only doing the will of the church, and hence of God.

Books, movies, and the popular media's exposure of the injustices of the Catholic Institution have served as the catalyst for thousands of adopted Irish children and their shamed mothers to come forward; for thousands of children sexually abused by pedophile priests in residential schools and parishes; for thousands of gay priests being used as scapegoats for the homophobic one percent, which denies the right of their gay clergy to own their truth; and for the thousands of victims of inquisitions, excommunications, financial embezzlements and laundering.

The one percent is quick to remind us of all the great charities and services they provide, which they generously do, but the bad seems to overshadow any humble good gestures.

It's only when we're able to say "Enough!" that we're prepared to transition emotionally, physically and spiritually.

AFTERWORD

As we are evolving into a spiritual, secularized society, many are leaving the structural framework of their faith communities and finding themselves without the support systems that were there for them, their families and often their own relationship with their Higher Power, however they understood that to be.

We've often left behind the laws and dogmas of our faith institution which offered us some happiness and inner peace. The Laws of the Universe that many spiritual writers such as Louise Hay, Dr. Wayne Dyer, Eckhart Tolle, Neville Garder are reminding us of, what were dismissed and belittled by many of us church men as too 'New Age' and seen as possible confusion and distraction to what we preached as the true faith.

As society becomes better educated and no longer willing to be subservient as we church men had trained the masses to be since the medieval era, many are left with a void for a sense of peace and happiness in the midst of demanding lifestyles, injustices and longings of the heart.

ABOUT THE AUTHOR

Before becoming a Roman Catholic priest, Ray Buteau's experiences led him to the Arctic Circle and Peace Corps work in Harlem, New York.

As a Priest, he took ASL studies at Gallaudet College and using his year in the Arctic as a guide, he published *Inuit' The People of Canada's Arctic* in 1978. In 1985 he had a key role in the establishment of Canada's first Catholic Bible College. After 17 years in parish ministry, he took advanced pastoral clinical training in spiritual care and served as a Spiritual Care Provider at Headingly Correctional Centre for the next eight years.

After leaving the priesthood in 2002, Ray developed 'Warrior of the Rainbow,' through which he offered spiritual counseling services in a non-religious context.

In 2012 *No Longer Lonely* was published and in 2015 *Those In Power*.

In 2017 a presentation for *No Longer Lonely* was completed using TED-talk outline criteria.

In 2018 a presentation for *Those In Power* was completed using TED-talk outline criteria.

Ray's goal in owning his truth as a gay former Catholic priest is to give a voice, and empowerment to many gay Roman Catholic priests, many in emotionally abusive relationships and many in the LGBTQ community.

He resides in Winnipeg, Manitoba Canada.

Ray Buteau may be contacted at

warrioroftherainbow@outlook.com

HEARTS to be HEARD

Giving a Voice to Creativity!

Wouldn't you love to help the physically, spiritually, and mentally challenged?

Would you like to make a difference in a child's life?

Imagine giving them:
confidence; self-esteem; pride; and self-respect.
Perhaps a legacy that lives on.

You see, that's what we do.
We give a voice to the creativity in their hearts,
for those who would otherwise not be heard.

Join us by going to

HeartstobeHeard.com

Help us, help others.

www.ingramcontent.com/pod-product-compliance
Lightning Source LLC
LaVergne TN
LVHW051239080426
835513LV00016B/1675